Survival 101

Bushcraft:

The Essential Guide for Wilderness Survival 2020

Rory Anderson

TABLE OF CONTENTS

INTRODUCTION

What you call bushcraft, others call survival. In the animal kingdom, humans are the only species who have completely eliminated their need to experience a connection to their survival, and it shows. Anywhere you look, you can easily find a society of humans who believe their food comes from the store, their homes come from landlords or the bank, and their means for survival comes from their employer. While this may be true for a modern society, when we get down into the nitty-gritty of survival, this mindset could cost you your life.

Bushcrafting is not a fad, nor is it exclusive to doomsdayers and other conspiracy theorists who believe the world is coming to an end. Bushcrafting is a selection of skills relevant to your survival, that can be used virtually anywhere in the world. When you learn how to preserve your livelihood through survival skills and strategies relevant to the human species, you are no longer at the mercy of our modern society and everything that comes with it. This means when things naturally go wrong, such as pandemics, natural disasters, or economic or political turmoil, you can rely on yourself to survive. With skills that help you survive, such as building shelter, feeding yourself in the wild, and preserving your health and safety, you no longer need to worry about anything that comes your way because you know, for wildfires, that you are prepared.

These days, there's no telling what will happen. Every year, new natural disasters rip through countries, destroying peoples' livelihood and wiping hundreds of thousands of people off the planet. Hurricanes, wildfires, pandemics, disease, and in some cases, even the government are all things you have to beware of when it comes to your survival. More than ever, we are seeing that living in urban environments is dangerous and that you are more likely to be exposed to threats if you live in an urban setting. During situations such as the coronavirus pandemic, for example, people in urban settings are exposed to moderate and extreme conditions, rather than the mild conditions being seen by less busy locales. This increased risk and exposure mean that you may well be required to leave your urban environment should anything go wrong and, if you do, you are going to need to know where to go and what to do once you get there. No matter what it may look like on the surface, we are all just animals looking to survive, and at the end of the day, you can only rely on *one* person to keep you alive – *You*.

Survival 101: Bushcraft is a tell-all book that includes everything you need to know to survive in the wild. From securing shelter and setting up camp to making a fire, navigating, trapping, tracking, and even making your own tools, we are going to cover everything you need to know to live safely and comfortably in the woods for any amount of time. While hobbyists can certainly gain knowledge here, this book was not written to supply some fad-driven industry of people who want to flaunt their knowledge. This book is written to help you survive, no matter what.

I suggest you study this book, keep it on hand, and maintain a hardcopy of it in your survival pack so that if you ever find yourself needing to take to the woods to survive, you have access to everything you need. One thing to know about the human condition is that, under pressure, our memories have a tendency to falter. Rather than placing all that demand on yourself in a circumstance that may already be the most stressful situation you ever face in your life, protect yourself by memorizing the contents of this book and keeping it handy just in case. You never know when you will need this knowledge.

Before you start reading, I want to say thank you for purchasing *Survival 101: Bushcraft*. I know many titles exist on this exact topic already, and I am grateful that you have chosen me to educate you on how to protect your livelihood and the livelihood of everyone you care about.

CHAPTER 1

What Skills Do You Need?

The remainder of this book is going to be focused on clear, step-by-step instructions on how to procure shelter, source, and capture food, and engage in everything else that is required of you in order for you to survive. Before we can get into any of that, though, you need to have a clear understanding of how to actually use any of this knowledge. Without any clear sense of direction or understanding in the order of things, you are going to find yourself struggling to put all of these pieces together to create the ability for you to survive.

Bushcrafting skills require you to control the three C's, core temperature, comfort, and convenience, using the five C's, cutting tools, cover elements, combustion devices, containers, and cordages. The skills you require include things such as making a fire, navigating the wilderness, trapping, foraging, building shelters, making tools, gathering supplies, and improvising as needed. With all of these things put together, you become far more likely to preserve yourself in the wilderness for as long as it is needed.

The Three C's

The 3 C's that are the most important to your survival include core temperature, comfort, and convenience. If either of these three C's are missed when it comes to preserving yourself in the wilderness, you are liable to falter and ultimately fail at surviving in the wild. Protecting these three elements must be your absolute main focus when it comes to establishing your wellbeing and increasing your likelihood of survival.

Core temperature is the primary element that you need to focus on immediately upon entering the wilderness. Especially if it is a cooler season, you need to secure a shelter that is going to be warm enough to maintain a livable body temperature. If your body temperature drops too low, your muscles will begin to stiffen, and it will become much more challenging for you to complete any of the necessary tasks in order to survive. You also run the risk of hypothermia or frostbite. Alternatively, if your body becomes too hot, your blood thickens and you run the risk of heatstroke or dehydration. Under either circumstance, your chances of survival drop drastically, so you need a shelter that helps you maintain a comfortable and manageable body temperature. You will also need clothes or garments you can wear that will provide you with the right body temperature anytime you are leaving the shelter. The clothes you choose, regardless of which climate they are for, need to be flexible enough that you can move around in them so that you can safely complete all of your tasks without your clothes impeding your success.

Your comfort is essential to survival because, to put it simply, without comfort, you begin to lose your will to live. Life may have its challenges and pitfalls, but if you are in a constant state of discomfort, you are going to find yourself coming up against massive amounts of mental, physical, and emotional stress. Physically, stress can damage your ability to maintain enough energy and strength to do everything that is required of you in order for you to survive. Mentally and emotionally, being in a constant state of distress will cause you to lose your will to carry on, which in and of itself can pose a threat to your survival. You must be willing and able to carry on by minimizing your stress as much as possible so that all of your energy can go toward your survival.

Finally, convenience is another essential factor. When you set things up in a way that makes them more convenient for you, you exert less energy into getting things done, which means you are more likely to experience greater levels of comfort. In addition to greater comfort levels, you are also using up fewer calories when things demand less of your energy, which means you do not have to gather as much food to keep up with your energy demands. Further, you can get more done with less amount of time because you are not investing so much into every single task that needs to get done. You will discover that surviving by your own two hands, rather than relying on grocery stores and carefully crafted supply chains, requires a lot more of your time. The more time you can save by making things convenient for yourself, the easier and more enjoyable it will be for you to survive.

The Five C's

The five C's are the tools that are required for you to control your three C's of survival. They include cutting tools, cover elements, combustion devices, containers, and cordages. If all you have are these five things in the wild, you will have plenty to get you started with. Everything else can be made or improvised, while these five things are much more challenging to improvise on and essential to virtually every aspect of surviving in the wilderness.

Cutting tools, including knives, axes, and shears, are all important to have in the wilderness. They will help you build your shelter, harvest and prepare your food, prepare fires, and do many other things that you will find to be essential to your survival. It is a good idea to have a variety of cutting tools on hand, each of which are easy for you to travel with so that you can rely on them as needed. With that being said, you are going to want to opt for multi-tools as they are often space savers, and they tend to be lighter to travel with. For example, a Swiss

Army knife is a great backwoods knife because it can do so many different things, and it is just one single piece of equipment.

Cover elements are useful for many reasons. Cover elements are used to build shelter, cover the ground to give you a cleaner and warmer space to live, and to cover your person so that you remain warm and safe when you leave your shelter. You will also use cover tools to cover and store your food, to pack things around in as needed, and to perform a myriad of other unexpected things when you are in the wilderness. Bringing along as many tarps and other cover elements as you reasonably can is ideal as it prevents you from having to harvest and tan several hides to build a shelter in. While there is room for improvising in the wilderness, you should still have some basic man-made cover elements, too.

Combustion devices are necessary as they allow you to start a fire. You may have seen different programs on TV where people strike flint and other elements together to make fire, and while this does work, it also takes a lot of time. Further, not every environment has minerals in it that are capable of starting fires. Ideally, you want to bring along as many matches as you possibly can, all in water-proof bags to prevent them from getting wet and not working any longer. You should also bring along lighters and lighter fuel, if possible, as they will be helpful in starting fires, too. Another excellent device that was recently developed is known as a permanent match, and it is a single tool that can be used over and over again to start a fire. This is a great tool to have on hand as it will help you keep your fire going for as long as possible.

Containers are useful in survival when it comes to storing food and water. You want containers that can be properly cleaned so that you are able to safely store everything inside of them without the worry of bacteria getting in and damaging the quality of your food or water. Ideally, you should use stainless steel containers as they can safely be boiled to eliminate bacteria, and are less likely to harbor bacteria in the first place. Plus, they are rust-resistant so they will last significantly longer. For water, purchasing a self-filtering water bottle is a good idea, too. Many survival stores sell self-filtering stainless steel water bottles that are capable of eliminating any contaminants from water found in the wilderness. This is a sure way to protect yourself against harmful bacteria that could lead to disease and, possibly, death. While plastic may seem easier and more accessible in our modern society, note that plastic harbors bacteria, and it cannot be boiled to clean it properly, which makes this a poor choice for bushcraft.

Cordages, or types of rope and cord, are important for your camp, too. You are going to want to bring along as much rope as you can in four different weights. You need a thread and needle for sewing, a lightweight nylon or paracord rope for hanging tarps and doing other similar tasks, a medium weight rope for building snares and traps, and a heavyweight rope for a variety of uses, from hanging food to helping you haul things around if need be. You should bring along as many lengths of each rope as is possible, as rope will always come in handy on a campsite.

The Order of Operations for Survival

Survival requires five basic things to be fulfilled: oxygen, water, food, shelter, and self-defense. When you can fulfill these five needs, you have everything you require in order to survive. Everything thereinafter is to create an easier means of survival for yourself. With that being said, if these five things are not fulfilled in the proper order, you will create vulnerabilities within yourself, which can threaten your survival. It is crucial that you follow the right steps to secure all five of these things as fast as possible, and as efficiently as possible so that you can guarantee your survival.

Although there are only five things that are required in order for you to survive, there are actually ten steps that need to be taken in order for you to survive. You must take these ten steps in order to ensure that you are ready to face the challenges that lie ahead of you. Understand that all ten of these things must be fulfilled in every single emergency, no matter how large or how small that emergency may seem. In some scenarios, you may be able to secure certain aspects of your survival through urban means, while in others, you may need to be solely responsible for procuring the supplies and building your own means of survival. You should be prepared to do whatever it takes, in any situation, to ensure your safety and the safety of anyone with you.

The first order of operations when it comes to survival is to get yourself in the mindset of surviving. When you first find yourself in a situation where you are solely responsible for your survival, it can come as a shock, and it can leave you feeling terrified, and even feeling like a victim of your circumstances. If you stay in this mentality, however, you are going to struggle to take charge and take the necessary action because you will be overridden by fear. As soon as you find yourself in a situation where you need to be responsible for your survival, you need to focus on staying as positive as you possibly can so that you can secure your means of survival. Positivity is going to boost your resiliency, your creativity, and your overall mental toughness so that it is easier for you to endure anything that comes your way.

The second order of operations is to render first aid. As you are leaving an urban environment, bring along as many first aid items as you possibly can. Ideally, you should have a fully equipped medical kit ready to go in case you ever find yourself in a survival setting, that way you can grab it and take it with you as a part of your supplies. We will discuss the exact tools you need in greater depth in Chapter 2: Tools You Need.

The third order of operations is to consider how you are going to defend yourself should anything go wrong. Knives and axes are incredibly helpful when it comes to self-defense. If you are capable of owning a gun and enough ammo and bringing it with you, this can be another great tool for self-defense. Be sure to use safety and transport of any sort of weaponry safely to avoid accidental injury or death.

The fourth order of operations is to make sure you have signals for every single person in your camp. While this will not necessarily be used third, before you leave an urban environment, you will want to secure whistles for each person who will be in your camp. As long as you can breathe, whistles will help you call for assistance to anyone else who may be in the bush with you, so they are important. This way, should you find yourself in danger or injured in the bush, you can signal to each other and receive prompt help.

Once you get into the bush itself, you reach the fifth order of operations. That is, to build a shelter. You need to build a shelter as fast as you possibly can, as nightfall will come, and temperatures will drop. While you can generally go about three days without water and about three weeks without food, it takes just a few hours for hypothermia and frostbite to settle in. Building a shelter will ensure that you have a safe, warm place to stay so that you do not find yourself exposed to the elements and damaging your potential to survive.

The sixth order of operation is to get water. You do not want to start a fire and then leave camp, and water will be needed rather quickly. If you were unable to bring any with you, you are going to want to find a safe water source like a stream, a river, or a waterfall to get water from. You are going to need to sterilize the water before drinking it, so unless you have a bottle that conditions water on the spot, wait until you are back at camp to safely do so.

The seventh order of operation is to build a fire. Once you are safely back at camp with your water, you can build yourself a fire so that you have warmth. Fire will also help you maintain light in the evening, boil water, cook food, and dry out your clothes if need be. You should have fire-starting materials on your person at all times so that if you ever get stuck away from the camp you have made; you can make yourself a fire. You should also have a fire going as often as possible at camp, ideally with someone there to tend to it to keep it from going out. It is easier to find wood to maintain a burning fire than it is to find more combustion tools to start a new one, so you want to preserve your fires for as long as possible to minimize your usage of combustion tools.

When shelter, water, and fire have been secured, you need to move on to food. Food is your eighth order of operations, and it should be found within 24-48 hours, especially since you will be stressed out, and your body needs food to help it remain resilient against everything you are up against. While you may be able to survive 3 weeks without food, the longer you go without it, the harder it will be to have enough energy to source any food. Food will be an all-consuming task since you are going to need to eat multiple times per day, so you should be ready to set up multiple means for securing food sources. Fishing, trapping, and foraging are all great places to start as they can provide you with easy access to nutritional food sources. When you are preparing your food, make sure you wash and cook it thoroughly to avoid accidentally ingesting any bacteria that may cause you to get sick, as curing sickness in the wilderness can be rather challenging, and it can pose a major threat to your survival.

The ninth order of operations is to keep yourself motivated. Especially if you are not used to having to be so hands-on with your survival, it can be easy to want to give up and throw in the towel. The amount of stress you face from a massive change in circumstances and the requirements of surviving can be exhausting and can prove to be a major burden. The longer you go on, the more you may wish to give up. This can worsen in the earliest hours of the morning, around 2 A.M., when your brain chemistry dips and pain levels become worse, and thoughts become darker and more challenging to face. If you can get yourself through the nights, getting through the days will be easier, and surviving will become more achievable.

The tenth order of business is to rescue yourself. In an ideal scenario, you would be able to use smoke signals to indicate where you are at so that a chopper can locate you, and you can be rescued. And, in some emergencies, that may still be required of you, so you will want to maintain a large enough fire that you can be located. If, however, you know that you are unlikely to be rescued, you are going to have to rescue yourself. This means that you are either going to need to find your way into a civilization where you can stay, or you are going to need to create your own civilization where you can stay indefinitely until things change. It may seem like an impossible thing to do, but where there is a will there is a way, and if you can stay on track with securing your survival, you will find a way.

CHAPTER 2
Tools You Need

Living in civilized society at present means that you have access to many tools that would be virtually impossible for you to source in the bush. Sourcing and storing tools that will aid in your survival is important, as it allows you to have everything handy should you find yourself in an emergency survival situation. In this chapter, we are going to discuss all of the different tools you should source and keep handy so that you can take these with you if need be. It is important that you get the best possible tools for yourself that are going to be the most useful in a survival situation. It is also important that you do not have too many things as you have to think in terms of practicality, including how practical it will be for you to transport everything. You want to bring only the most necessary things so that you can survive, as you will be able to source everything else from the bush.

When it comes to bushcrafting, you'll note that there is no "one" tool in any given category that is *the* best. Rather, there are many great tools out there, and you are going to need to find the ones that are most accessible for you. Get the best of what you can afford, and the one that is going to be easiest for you to handle and make use of, while also having the strength and longevity it needs to endure life outdoors for extended periods of time. That way, you know you are investing your money in a worthy investment.

Packs

Packs are a crucial tool when it comes to bushcrafting. You need a pack that is going to give you enough room for all of your supplies, while also distributing the weight evenly across your back so that it is easy for you to carry those supplies. Packs made for bushcrafting have an ergonomic aspect to them to make them easier to carry for longer periods of time, and they are made to be hardy and lightweight so that they can endure the bush without adding excess pounds to your luggage.

There are ten different elements you are going to need to consider when it comes to buying the right pack, and these elements are best looked for in person so that you can feel confident in the pack you are buying. With that in mind, do your best to avoid purchasing your pack online as it could lead to an expensive and poor quality purchase.

First, you need to consider the size of the back that you need. Hobbyists and weekend campers can get away with smaller packs, but if you plan on surviving in the woods for any period of time, you are going to need as large of a pack as you can manage. If you have other members of your household that will be coming with you, you want to fit each of them with a pack they can carry, too, so that you can transport more with you.

Next, you need to consider where the frames are within the pack. External frames are old-school packs that were used by previous generations, though they are not as popular as they once were because they can cause pressure sores on the various areas where they touch the body. However, they do allow you to carry more inside of the pack and strap gear outside of the pack because of where they are situated. Internal frames, on the other hand, may be more comfortable to carry, but they do take up more space in the pack and eliminate your ability to strap as many things to the outside of your pack. Another thing to consider is where you are likely to end up. External frames can be bulkier, so if you think you will end up in overgrown brush, an internal frame would be better as it will be easier for you to carry through the bush.

Hip belt and shoulder padding are important features to consider. The majority of the weight of your pack will sit on your hips, and much of it will be in your shoulders, too. Packs with added padding in these two areas can be more comfortable to carry, especially if you suspect you will need to carry them for a long way, as they will relieve some of the pressure off of your hips and shoulders.

Proper ventilation on a bushcraft pack is important, no matter what weather you think you are likely to be in when you are carrying your pack. Your pack will create heat against your back, and in warmer conditions, this will be especially uncomfortable. This heat can also lead to sweating and sores, which can both be dangerous, depending on the situation. A properly ventilated pack should be made of mesh, which will help you regulate body temperature more efficiently.

External attachments are essential when it comes to a pack that will be used in survival circumstances. External attachments ensure you can strap more to your pack as needed so that you can carry more with you. Look for a pack with a variety of external attachments so that if you need them, you have them.

Bushcraft packs need to be well-organized when you pack them so that you can find everything easily, so you need a pack that has different access points and organized compartments. With that being said, packs with more compartments can be more expensive, so don't go overboard. Buy what you can afford, as you can always take care of organization through other methods later on, such as using smaller storage bags inside.

Especially if you live in a wet climate, you are going to want a pack with a rain cover. With core temperature being as important as it is, the last thing you want is to arrive at camp and have everything too wet for use. A rain cover will keep everything inside your pack dry. You can either buy a pack that has one built-in, or you can buy a separate rain cover for your pack. Be sure to keep it in an easily accessible spot in case you need to use it.

Packs with removable lids are handy as these lids can help you store more within the pack, but they can also be removed and left behind to reduce weight as needed. If you will be living in the bush for an extended period of time, this is helpful as you can offload many of your belongings at camp and pack just what you need for shorter trips away from camp, such as when you are hunting or fishing for the day.

Built-in water reservoirs can be extremely helpful in packs, especially if you are able to fill your pack with water before you leave your home. This way, you have safe drinking water as you prepare camp for the days, weeks, or months ahead. If your pack does not have a hydration system in it, do your best to fill water bottles and pack them before leaving so that you have access to clean, fresh drinking water.

Finally, you need to check that the pack fits you. Packs come in all shapes and sizes, and some are going to fit while others will not. Try the pack on, put some weight in it, and walk around a bit to see if it is comfortable. Finding a pack that fits you properly is important, as a well-fit pack is easier to carry for longer periods of time. This way, you are able to preserve your comfort and your energy levels, making bushcraft much easier for you.

Cutting Tools

Cutting tools are essential in a survival situation. You will use them to cut down branches to help build your camp, to chop wood so you can build fires, to cut your tying tools with, to cut your food with, and to do so many other things with. Proper knives, axes, and saws, as well as sharpening tools, will be important for your camp. Ideally, you should have the following four types of cutting tools: a Swiss Army knife, a buck knife, an ax, and a saw. If you can bring a machete or a similar size knife with you, this will also be helpful. You can add more knives if you feel it is needed, such as ones to eat with or additional knives for additional members who will be coming with you. Otherwise, these will be enough to keep you going.

Swiss Army Knife

Swiss Army knives, with all of their ends and attachments, are useful when bushcrafting. Ensure you buy a high-end Swiss Army knife with a proper grip on it made of high-quality wood or stainless steel to ensure that it is likely to last. Low-quality knives like ones made of plastic will fall apart quickly, rendering them useless. Ideally, every adult member of your camp should have a Swiss Army knife as they can be used for so many things.

Buck Knife

Buck knives are great for hunting, particularly when it comes to butchering the animals you harvest. A buck knife is a heavier duty knife that can be used for many purposes as well, including cutting thicker ropes with, cutting smaller branches with, or even whittling branches into arrowheads so they can be used to spear fish if needed. While a buck knife with a fixed handle may be more durable, one that can be flipped closed for storage is safer to carry around in a pack. If you get one with a fixed handle, be sure to get a proper sheath to avoid accidentally cutting yourself on the knife.

Axe

Axes are great when it comes to building camp, and building fires. You will be able to cut back smaller pieces of wood as well as make firewood as needed. In the event of an emergency, axes can also be wielded as a weapon in case of a wild animal invasion on your campsite.

Saw

Saws will be excellent for building camp. With a saw, you can cut back pieces of wood and fashion them into various shapes to help you build shelters, tables, chairs, and other camp necessities. They are excellent building tools, and therefore are incredibly handy to have on a campsite. You should have a single-handled saw that is large enough to cut through large logs, but small enough to transport into the bush. Make sure the blade is cut of stainless steel or a similar metal to ensure they are rust-proof, as you will want your saw to last a long time. As well, opt for a handle made of treated wood or comfortable metal so that it will last in the bush, too.

Machete

If you will be going into an overgrown forested area, a machete is an excellent tool to use to help you whack back branches and carve out paths for yourself. You can also use it to cut back any overgrowth that may be growing into your campsite. As well, machetes can be used as a weapon when needed, so it is a good idea to keep it close by, especially when you are sleeping. This way, if you find yourself under attack, you can protect yourself and your campsite.

Grind

Grinds are a sharpening tool that can be used to sharpen any knife blade as needed. It is a good idea to keep a grind on hand at all times so you can sharpen your blade, as sharp blades are less dangerous than dull or chipped blades. Grinds are generally an easier sharpening tool to use, as they have a cutout in them where the knife is inserted to perform the sharpening process. You should have at least one for your campsite.

Whetstone

Whetstones are another type of sharpening tool that can be used to help sharpen any blades you have with you at your campsite. With whetstone, you will need to first dampen it, and then you will need to drag the blade on a 15-degree angle back toward yourself, with the sharp end of the blade pointed away from you. This will help you sharpen the knife and clean off any chips that may occur on the sharp edge of the knife, thus keeping your knife safe to be used.

Tying Tools

Tying tools will be used for everything from creating snares and safely storing food above the ground, to tying up tarps and tying branches together to create shelter. Tying tools can also be used to tie pelts and hides together so that you can create more cover elements, or even to help carry things through the woods. These incredibly versatile tools come in handy more than you might expect, so you will need a healthy variety for your campsite.

Rope

Because of how much tying you will be doing in the bush, it is important that you have tying materials that are strong, durable, and easy to work with. Layered sisal rope is a great option for rope, as is paracord. While neither will be functional for climbing purposes, they will both be strong enough to perform many other duties that assist in your survival.

For climbing purposes, you want something that is around 9.5mm and made of something that is intended for climbing. Generally, climbing ropes are made of nylon fibers that are wound tightly together, and they feature a nylon sheath, so that they are strong, durable, and can be rubbed against any surface without tearing and dropping you in the process.

Cordage

Cordage varies from rope to rope in that it is made of a set of ropes and cords, while ropes are made of thick strings and fibers that come together to make them stronger. Paracord, Dyneema, and ultra-high molecular weight polyethylene (UHMWPE) are all great cordages that can be used in your camp for a variety of purposes. Nylon cords are also great as, much like with climbing rope, they are made in such a way that causes them to be incredibly durable.

Snare Wire

Snare wire is a specific type of wire that is used to create snares which are used to catch small mammals such as rabbits and hares. This wire is thin and clear so that animals cannot see it, and it is set in areas where the animals are likely to run through so that as they run through, the snare catches them. Once they are caught by the snare, they will pass away, which will make harvesting them and bringing them back to camp easier.

Lashing, Bindings, and Toggles

Lashing, bindings, and toggles are actually skills rather than specific tools; however, they are used as tools when it comes to bushcrafting. All three of these skills are forms of knot skills that use cordage and rope to help you create a certain desired effect with your rope. Lashing is a rope strategy that forms a web of sorts that connects a variety of things together, such as large branches for a fence or for shelter. Lashing is not so much of a true knot form as a wrap that is used to hold things together. Binding is similar to lashing, except it contains fewer wraps because it is only intended to hold something snuggly together, like a true knot. Finally, toggles are a moveable crosspiece that is used to connect or fasten something together. A simple example of a toggle would be if you were to make yourself a poncho and connect it at the front by a rope loop on one side with a small stick on the other side that would be inserted through the rope loop to hold both ends of the poncho together. These toggles can be used in a variety of different methods in bushcraft and can be made in a variety of different sizes, too.

Cooking Tools

Securing food is going to be an ongoing process when you are in the bush, and so is cooking that food since you are going to need to be absolutely confident that your food is safe to eat. Especially when it comes to game meat, you need to ensure that the meat is thoroughly cooked all the way through every single time to avoid ingesting anything that could contain diseases or parasites, which would make you sick and possibly kill you.

Containers

You will see a great deal about what types of containers to use for bushcraft, ranging from different types of plastic containers to plastic bags and even old plastic food containers such as clean plastic peanut butter jars. While these may be effective for hobbyists or short term bushcrafters, they will not be ideal for long term survival as they can quickly become filled with bacteria and challenging to properly cleanse in the bush.

Stainless steel food containers and water canteens or other metal containers with properly securing lids that are completely rust resistant and capable of tolerating high temperatures are best when it comes to storing food. These types of containers can easily be boiled for sterilization so that they can be reused over and over again. Glass can also be used, though it will be heavier and a little more dangerous to transport due to the fact that it could break. As well, if a glass container cracks, you will not be able to use it any longer as the cracks will harbor bacteria.

Pots and Pans

Cast iron and stainless steel cookware are the best options when you are living in the bush. Be mindful that cast iron can be rather heavy, so bringing along only one or two cast iron cookware items is ideal to avoid having to carry anything excessive into the bush. Stainless steel pots are excellent as they can handle virtually anything, can be properly sterilized, and will not rust in the bush.

Avoid anything with a non-stick coating, as non-stick coatings break down over an open flame, and over certain temperatures. They can quickly contaminate your food and cause you to become sick, which is obviously not ideal.

In addition to pots and pans, you may want to get yourself a cast-iron kettle, or a stainless steel kettle that you can take with you. While water can be boiled in a pot for drinking purposes, boiling it in a kettle makes it easier to pour into your drinking containers.

Utensils

Cooking utensils are important when it comes to bushcraft as you do not want to risk putting your hands anywhere near hot water, hot cookware, or hot food. Burns may seem minor in an urban environment, but in the bush, they can quickly become infected which can lead to a life-threatening situation.

Wooden and rust-resistant metal utensils are optimal. Choose barbecue-sized utensils when it comes to tongs, spatulas, and other cookware that will be used directly over the fire as they will afford you more space between your hand and the flame. Select a few different types of spoons, tongs, a spatula, and a stainless steel mesh sieve for your bushcraft utensils. You should also bring along a pair or two of oven mitts, though keep in mind that they need to be used very cautiously around the fire as they can catch fire, and they only work up to certain temperatures.

Another cooking tool you may wish to have on hand is a large metal S hook. When cooking in the bush, your oven mitts may not be useful, and you are going to need a way to remove your pots from the oven. An S hook can be inserted through a handle and used to carefully remove a hot pot or pan from the top of your oven, so long as there is not too much inside of that pot or pan which could lead to splashing and burns.

Serving Ware

As with the rest of your cookware, stainless steel serving ware is the best option as it gives you the ability to properly sterilize your dishes between meals. Only bring one plate, one bowl, and one fork, spoon, and knife per person camping with you. You might bring one additional set just in case, but otherwise, you will be wasting space and weight on serving ware. Be sure to clean them thoroughly between meals to avoid contamination and sickness.

Body Coverage Tools

When it comes to surviving in the bush, it can be easy to think about what tools you will need to help you build shelter, harvest food, and cook the food. However, you may not think about clothing until the last minute. Nonetheless, clothing is imperative as you need clothes that are going to help you maintain the proper body temperature while also being practical and useful. As with everything else, you want to avoid bringing too much, so opt for clothes that are going to be functional and practical when it comes to survival situations.

Daytime Clothes

For daytime clothes, you will want two pairs of pants, two short sleeve shirts and two long sleeve shirts, a proper survival jacket, at least three pairs of underpants, and eight pairs of long socks.

For your pants, opt for khaki cutoff style pants that can easily be transformed into a pair of shorts, as this will help you maintain your temperature in both hot and warm climates without taking up nearly as much space in your pack.

For your jacket, opt for one that has an inner shell that can be removed and used as a sweater on days when an entire jacket may be too heavy. The outer shell of your jacket should have plenty of pockets that you can use to store various survival items, ranging from a small on-the-go first aid kit to snacks and your Swiss Army knife.

For your socks, opt for four pairs of cotton socks for hotter days and four pairs of wool socks for cooler days. Packing plenty of socks is important as these are the first clothing items to wear down in the bush due to all of the walking you will be doing, so you want plenty of extras.

For everything else, opt for breathable yet durable clothes made of cotton. Avoid clothing brands that are known for quickly breaking down and opt instead for brands that can withstand the outdoors so that your clothing is more likely to last you. Making your own clothes in the bush can be rather challenging, so you want to avoid finding yourself in any such situation.

If you are going to be in a particularly cool climate, you may also want to bring a pair or two of thermal underwear, which can be worn under your clothes for added warmth. Thermal underwear made of a wool blend will be best as it will be breathable while also helping to keep you warm.

Sleepwear

Your sleepwear should always be separate from your daytime clothes, as you want something clean, dry, and warm to sleep in. Not only will this support you with survival, but it will also help boost morale by helping you feel more comfortable when you rest. Thermal underwear is a great choice for sleeping, though light cotton pants and shirts can be used, too. You should opt for full pants and long sleeves with your sleepwear, as this will help ensure that you are keeping yourself protected. Exposed skin is exposed to bugs that can carry bacteria and disease, so you want to avoid being exposed whenever possible.

In addition to actual clothes, be sure to bring a sleeping bag for each person that will be staying with you. You will want to get one that is durable, and that can withstand cold temperatures so that if you find yourself out below freezing, you will have everything you need to survive.

Camp Coverage Tools

Coverage for your camp is equally as important as coverage for your body, as it will give you an extra layer of protection from the elements. While much of your coverage can be crafted from brush and branches, having man-made coverage tools can help ensure that your camp is far more protected by offering better shade and water protection.

Tarps

Tarps will always be helpful when you are bushcrafting. Ideally, you should have one small, one medium, and one large tarp. You may also want to bring one additional small tarp to be used for patchwork on your other three tarps, should they begin to tear. Otherwise, the small tarp can be used over small areas, or it can be used to help protect your food reserves. Medium and large tarps can be used in the building of actual shelters to minimize your exposure to the eliminates.

You want to avoid using brightly colored tarps as they can attract attention to your camp and encourage unwanted animals to visit you. Instead, choose neutral colors that will blend in with the environment you will be in so that you can protect yourself from wildlife.

Ground Cloths

Ground cloths are used to help protect you from the elements below you. The ground itself can harbor bugs, bacteria, and a lot of moisture, especially if you are in a more humid or wet climate. Bringing along ground cloths can protect you from those elements by giving you a layer of protection between yourself and the bare ground.

You can choose tarps for ground cloth, though you will also want to have warmer, thicker options to place over your tarps. While tarps will keep away moisture and provide an additional layer to protect you from bugs, waxed canvas and animal hides are also great. Waxes canvas aids in protecting you against moisture in the ground while also providing an additional layer for warmth, while animal hides will add warmth and cushion, particularly for areas where you will be sleeping.

Rain Covers

Tarps are great for rain covers, though waterproof canvas, nylon, felt, and polyester are all great, too. These are all materials that are commonly used to make waterproof tents with, and they can be used for a number of things from keeping yourself dry to keeping areas of your camp protected from the rain. If you have enough space in your pack, and you know you live in a climate that is generally wet, these materials can be used to cover common walkways in your camp to keep you dry from place to place. For example, between your sleeping shelter and your cleaning shelter. This way, you are able to keep yourself dry and comfortable the entire way. Again, choose neutral colors that will not attract any attention from neighboring wildlife.

Fire Tools

Fire is essential to survival, so you are going to want to pack plenty of things to help you aid in building and maintaining fires in your camp. Combustion tools as well as starter materials will be important as they all provide you with what you need to create and maintain a fire. Actual firewood can be harvested from the bush itself, so do not worry about that.

Combustion Tools

In bushcraft, there are three types of combustion tools you can use: matches, lighters, and permanent matches. Matches are often inexpensive and are easy to travel with, so pack as many as you can, as well as match striking material so you can start your matches. Be sure to store them in a double-wrapped, heavy-duty waterproof zip-locked bag to avoid any moisture getting into your matches.

Lighters are also great for bushcraft, though they can die out once the fuel has been used up, so you may want to keep added fuel on hand. Barbecue lighters, as well as cigarette lighters, are best for bushcraft, as barbecue lighters can be used for larger fires in your camp while cigarette lighters can be used for smaller ones when you travel away from camp, such as for hunting.

Permanent matches are devices that were made specifically for bushcrafting, and they are designed to start your fire over and over again without requiring anything aside from the permanent match itself. Keeping one or two on hand is an excellent choice for bushcrafting as they are reliable, efficient, and can be used for a long time, while matches and lighters will eventually run out.

Fire Starting Materials

When you want to get a good fire going, you are going to need a lot more than some well-placed logs to get you started. You need materials that are going to quickly catch fire so that you can keep the fire going long enough to catch your wood on fire. Cotton, dryer lint, pine cones, wood shavings, and dry grass are all excellent fire-starting materials that are lightweight and easy to travel with, and some of them can even be found right there in the bush. You will want to keep plenty on hand so you can start and maintain your fires as needed.

Other Camp Tools

There are a few additional camp tools you should have on hand that will help you survive in the bush for any period of time. These tools may not belong to any particular category, but they are important to your survival.

Compass

A good lensatic compass for bushcrafting is one that is properly set and reliable. You may even wish to have two on hand to ensure that you are able to keep exact track of yourself while you are traveling away from camp. Choose a functional and practical compass made of a rust-resistant metal that will work for years to come, and practice using it, so you know exactly what to do when it comes time to rely on it.

You should also keep several pieces of paper and writing tools on hand, including pencils and colored pencil crayons, as you can use them to help you create a map of your surroundings so that you know exactly where you are at all times. Keeping track will be important, as you never want to venture so far away that you end up lost and without any of your survival tools.

First Aid Kit

Your first aid kit should be filled with gloves, drugs, and medications, antiseptic wipes, minor wound and blister kits that include gauze, steri-strips, a suture kit, wound dressing pads, plasters, compeed, and a thermometer, a crepe bandage, a military dressing or two, a nasopharyngeal airway, a syringe, a blunt needle, a CPR mask, small bandages, transpore tape, Betadine, benzoin, a temporary cavity or tooth filling, superglue, tweezers, safety pins, a whistle, sheers, a lighter, and a head-torch. If you have a child on hand or access to one or two diapers, you should include these in your medical kit, too, as they are excellent for absorbing blood should a more intense wound be sustained. You should also have a write up of important usage factors, such as any important information on the drugs and medications, and instructions on how to use the plasters and apply the bandages. This way, you know exactly what to do and how to use them without causing damage to the person you are applying these tools on.

Other Tools

In addition to everything previously mentioned, you will want to bring anything else you can that will help you with survival. Binoculars, fishing line, and hooks, a shovel, baskets, additional filters for water filtration, flares, a radio, solar-powered flashlights, a small sewing kit with extra sewing needles, a mallet, and a metal grate for cooking on top of are all great tools to have on hand, also.

CHAPTER 3

Making A Shelter And Setting Up Camp

As you know, the first order of operations upon arriving in your area of intended survival is to set up camp. You are going to need a single shelter, first, which will be used as a primary shelter for sleep, storing your belongings, and changing your clothes, as well as hiding away from the elements as needed. After you have built your initial shelter, you will go on to create any additional shelters you need for your camp, ranging from a separate place to store your goods, a place to safely store your foods, a place to cook, and a place to practice hygiene.

The Five W's of Picking Your Campsite

Where you set up camp is just as important as how you set up camp, as the location of your camp will aid in convenience and comfort, as well as your ability to maintain a proper core temperature. There are five W's that you need to consider when it comes to picking the right campsite, including water, waste, weather, widowmakers, and wildlife.

Your camp should be close to water so that you can easily haul water back to camp without having to trek too far to get it. However, you do not want to be so close to water that you run the risk of being caught in a flood zone. Look for a spot that will be higher than the water itself, yet close enough that it is easy for you to access.

Waste removal will be important for your campsite as it ensures hygiene while also keeping possible wildlife attractants away from you. Ideally, you should pick a waste removal spot that will allow you to easily package and remove waste from the woods when you are ready to leave. However, that may not be practical if you will be surviving there for an extended period of time.

31

For that reason, simply choose somewhere farther away and easy to access. As well, make sure your waste is not upstream from where you are, and that it is not at risk of contaminating your water in its final location.

Weather is one of your biggest risk factors when it comes to survival, regardless of how nice the weather seems. It can turn fast, and any type of weather can be particularly challenging to navigate when you are exposed. Pick an area that offers natural shelter, and that will not run the risk of exposure to things such as wind and precipitation.

Widowmakers are a type of tree. Specifically, they are a dead tree that is already beginning to dry off and rot. A strong gust of wind or any heavy precipitation can lead to these trees falling over, which can be incredibly dangerous for your camp. In some instances, they have even been responsible for major injury and death. You want to beware that there are no widowmaker trees in your area. You should also look for other possible disasters that could occur, such as rock slides, which would threaten your survival. Avoid setting up camp anywhere that would expose you to natural threats.

Wildlife is an inevitable part of the bush, and you are going to need to know how to protect yourself from them when it comes to survival. One thing to know with wildlife is that there are certain areas where they frequent, and other areas where they don't spend much time. You can tell busy areas from non-busy areas based on the amount of scat, footprints, and other tell-tale signs that wildlife has been around, such as broken brush, worn-in paths, and scratches in trees. You should also pay attention to wasps nests or hornets nests, ants nests, or anything else that could be dangerous to be situated around. Naturally, you want to stay away from these areas to avoid putting yourself in an area that is highly likely for you to become exposed to plenty of wildlife. As well, you want to consider how well your camp is set up for you to protect yourself from wildlife, such as how easy it will be to safely store your food away from camp.

Building Your Main Shelter

If you arrive at your camp late, you may only have time to build a small shelter from smaller branches and twigs nearby, as well as any tarps and groundcovers you have already brought with you. As soon as you can, however, you want to get on with making a proper shelter that you can stay in. This will require larger branches to construct a frame; then you will require items that can be used to build a roof. Dry hogweed logs, long grass or cane, spruce (not fir) needle branches or ferns, leaves, and moss are all great for constructing the top of your shelter. If you have a tarp you brought along with you, you can also use that in your roof to create a stronger layer of protection. Other materials that can be used to construct your shelter include snow, clay, bark, flat stones, and even trash.

When building your shelter, you will want to have your axe and saw handy so that you can shape your frame branches as needed, and cut things down if necessary to get them to fit into place. Your tarp, rope, and knife will also be handy to help you haul things back to camp, and a bucket and shovel will come in handy if you are using snow or clay to construct your shelter.

The easiest way to build your main shelter is to find a spot in your camp where you can naturally be sheltered. For example, if you see a dugout in the side of a rock form, a few trees huddled together, or even a hollowed-out fallen tree, you can use this as the basis for your shelter. Of course, check the safety of this space to ensure that you are not at risk of anything falling and hurting you, and to be sure that animals are not already using that shelter.

If you cannot find a natural spot with shelter, you will want to make the next best thing: an A-frame shelter. While there are many types of shelters you can build in the bush, these are simple and durable. You will build an A-frame shelter by cutting thick branches to construct an A-frame and then building your roof on top of that. For an A-frame shelter, you will want 5 Y-shaped branches and one long branch that is about 1.25 times the length of your body. You will use the Y-shape branches to prop up the larger one, which will form the peak of your roof. Avoid making your A-frame shelter too large, as they can become more at risk of being damaged by the weather if they are too big, and the branches themselves can pose a threat to your safety. Instead, keep it nice and cozy so that you are tucked safely away and so that you are able to keep yourself comfortable and warm throughout the night.

When you build your shelter, you always want to build it from the ground up. You will start with your ground cover; then, you will build your frame, then you will build out your roof. A roof should be started with a layer of branches that will provide a frame for you to add everything else to. You can use lashings and bindings to help keep everything secured and in place. Below you will find the description of some common rope techniques that you can use for camp setup. If you are using a tarp, you would add it in next. Then, you would use spruce needle branches, leaves, long grasses, or even clay to construct the rest of your roof. Make it as packed as you possibly can to avoid any leaks which would get water into your shelter.

Building Additional Shelters

In addition to your main shelter, you may want to construct additional shelters for your camp, depending on how long you will be staying. If your sleeping shelter is particularly small, you may wish to create a shaded shelter where you can sit during the day to relax and get away from the weather. This shelter can also be used as a safe place for you to prepare food and construct things for camp without bringing anything into your main sleeping shelter.

Another shelter you may want to have in your camp is a hygiene shelter. A hygiene shelter can be used for washing yourself, but it can also be used as a sort of first aid spot in your camp, providing you with a clean space to sit down and tend to any cuts, scrapes, bruises, or anything else you may have received during the day. This shelter can be small and should be kept clean at all times. It should also have a proper log or something to sit on so that the person being treated can sit safely up and away from the ground and any contaminants on the ground. Your hygiene shelter should be close to water and a fire so that you can sterilize any equipment that may need to be used during a first aid situation.

Tarp Setup

Setting up a tarp for your camp can be done in a variety of ways, depending on what you need and what size your tarp is. The terrain you are setting up in will also affect the way you set up your tarp. The four easiest ways to set up a tarp include flying a tarp, building a lean to, setting up a diamond shelter, and creating tarp tents. You will also need to consider your ground cloth to ensure that your tarp is properly insulated.

Flying a Tarp

To fly a tarp means that the edges do not touch the ground at all, creating more of a shelter over top of you. This is excellent for day shelter, or for shelter in hot areas where a tent-style shelter may be too hot to sleep in. To fly a tarp, you are going to need five lengths of rope, including one that is longer then the tarp is wide. You will set up your tarp between two trees that are relatively close together, but far enough apart that your tarp will stretch between the two of them without wrinkling or folding over. Then, you will take your longest length of rope and tie it around the trunk of one tree about 5-6 feet high, and then tie it at the same height on the other tree, pulling it taut. Next, you will toss the tarp over the taut rope so that it hangs down with half on either side. Then, you will take your four additional lengths of rope and tie them into the corners of each tarp and attach them to something nearby, such as a low stump or a sturdy branch on some nearby brush. Your tarp should look like a tent that has been raised in the air.

Tarp Tent

A tarp tent is made with a single tarp and is used to keep you sheltered from the elements. While it will not keep you warm in the cold, it will keep you away from cold winds and rains. You can then stuff the tent with insulating layers of sleeping bags, clothes, and ground cloth as needed. For your tarp tent, you will want one tarp, one tree, and one branch that has been removed from a tree. The branch should be thick enough that it will be able to stand on its own. Then, you will need string and stakes, or nearby underbrush that you can tie your tent to if stakes aren't available. You will set up your tent by first locating the center of the tarp along one side and tying that to the tree, about 4 feet high. Make it a bit lower if you have a smaller tarp, or a bit higher if you have a larger one. Then, you are going to set your branch upright a few feet away from the tree. You want it far enough away that you will have a decent shelter, but close enough that the back end of your tarp will reach the ground even once it's been draped over the branch. Next, you are going to drape the tarp over the branch and then tie or stake down the edges so that they stay neatly tucked in on the ground. If you have no stakes, you could use rocks in a pinch.

Tarp Lean-To

The tarp lean to shelter is another shelter that can easily be made using two trees that are nearby. The trees should be far enough apart that you can keep your tarp taut when tying it up. The nice thing about a lean to shelter is that it will not require the long length of rope to hold up the middle like flying a tarp will. To create your lean-to, you will simply tie one corner of the tarp to one tree and one to another. Then, with the other two corners, you can either tie them to the ground, stake them to the ground, or hold them down with heavy rocks. The result should be a tarp that is hung tightly between two trees and able to be sat under, lied under, or used to keep your gear dry.

Diamond Shelter Tarp

A diamond shelter tarp is a fly technique that allows you to fly your tarp while still getting good protection out of it. These are great for protecting you from rain or wind, and they can also be used for sleeping inside. To make your diamond shelter tarp, you will need three lengths of rope, or one length of rope and three stakes or heavy rocks to hold down the corners. The best spot to create your diamond shelter tarp will be somewhere where there is a tree you can tie it to, and where there is a low stump, branch, or tree, you can attach the other side to. You will take your long length of rope and attach it to the tree about 3-4 feet up the trunk. Then, you will tie the other end of the rope to the ground, or to a stake in the ground if you have one. You will then place the tarp over the rope diagonally so that one corner touches the tree trunk, and the opposite corner touches the ground. The other two corners will need to be staked to the ground or held in place with heavy rocks.

Ground Cloth

Ground cloth is essential for your tents as it helps insulate them and keep you warm. A proper ground cloth will keep moisture out and body heat in, effectively warming up your tent so that you do not catch a chill or endanger your precious core temperature. Ground cloth should be set corner to corner at the bottom of your tent so that you are able to keep as much heat in as possible. If you are in a hot climate and you are not using a carefully closed in shelter, you can lay a ground cloth under your sleeping bag and then sleep in, or on, the sleeping bag. Even in a drier climate, this is important as you do not want to get any moisture in your clothes. Once you get damp in the bush, it is hard to dry off, and being damp for too long can be very bad for your skin and your health.

Lashes, Bindings, and Toggles

Making lashes, bindings, and toggles are all essential skills to have if you are going to be surviving in the bush. These teach you how to make sure that your rope actually stays where you place it, effectively keeping your tools in place. The easiest techniques to learn that will also get you the furthest in the bush include square lashing, snowshoe binding, and making a basic toggle.

Square Lashing

To do square lashing, you are going to place your two items you are connecting so that they are perpendicular to each other, with a cross in the center. They will end up at a 90-degree angle once tied. For the sake of easier explaining, let's imagine you have two sticks perpendicular to one another, and you are tying them together with a square lashing. You will start by tying a knot around the bottom stick, nice and close to where the two sticks cross. Then, you will pull your rope up and over the top stick, then down and under the other side of the bottom stick, opposite of where you tied the knot. Then, you will come up around and over the top stick, opposite to the side where you went over the last time. Now, you will go under where you placed your knot. You will continue weaving over and under until you have done this three times around. Then, you will wrap all the way around the top stick next to the knot and go in the reverse direction three times. When you are done, you will tie the rope in place with a simple knot.

Simple Binding

When you are binding something together, such as one log to another, you want to make sure you do it in such a way that it is held tightly in place and won't move. This method is important if you are going to be attaching logs together so that you can form them into a roof over your shelter, or sides for your shelter. You will bind by first taking the center of a length of rope and wrapping it around a piece of wood completely so that you have one full wrap and two equal tail lengths. Then, you will wrap it completely around the piece of wood you want to attach it to before wrapping it all the way around the bottom or original piece again and coming back up either side. You will now pull it tight. If you are connecting heavier branches or logs, you will want to do this one to two more times, depending on the thickness of the branches or logs. Then, you will start wrapping them around completely but pulling them down the length of the log as you go, creating long "x" shapes across the log. When you reach the middle, you will wrap one complete circle in place. Then, you will make "x" shapes again until you reach the other end of the branch or log. There, you will make one to three tight, complete wraps again. Then, you will tie off.

Making a Toggle

Making a toggle when you are In the bush is incredibly simple. All you will do is find a sturdy material that is somewhat thin and about 2-3" wide. You want to pick something that will be steady and not break, such as a thick branch, a rock, a piece of metal, or even a piece of a larger animal's femur bone. You will then tie a piece of rope around the very center of that item. You can now insert your toggle into the grommets on your tarp to hold it up, use it to keep a rope wrapped snuggly around a tree without tying it, or even use it to hold things in your pack. It you have nothing to insert the toggle into, make a simple knot on your rope with a loop in it and insert the toggle into the loop. This will keep everything nice and tight and secure. If you are securing something heavier or larger, always use thicker, sturdier toggles to avoid having the toggle snap, and someone gets injured as a result.

Hygiene, Organization, and Protection

Keeping your camp hygienic, organized, and protected is of utmost importance. Proper hygiene will ensure that no one gets sick, organization will ensure that you can find everything you need the moment you need it, and protection will keep you safe from the elements and wildlife.

Personal hygiene can be achieved using a few methods. When you cannot safely wash in running water, consider taking a smoke bath. By lighting a fire and bathing in the smoke, the smoke kills any bacteria on your body, which effectively cleanses you. As well, the smell is less likely to attract bugs such as flies and mosquitoes. If you can find oak, hickory, birch, aspen, or poplar trees, you can take some of their bark and boil it until the water becomes dark. As soon as the water is of a manageable temperature, dip a cloth in and wash your body with the all-natural tannin body wash. For your teeth, you can use twigs from dogwood or sassafras trees, which are both useful for cleaning and excellent because they have tannic acid, which will help cleanse your teeth, much like how it helps cleanse your body. Chew up the small twigs as this is how they become fibrous and work well as toothbrushes. If you need to wash your hands, such as after dealing with an animal carcass, you will want to find a yucca plant or a yarrow plant, as both can be scrubbed across your hands to cleanse them. Avoid ingesting these plants; however, yucca, in particular, is poisonous if ingested, but it is harmless on your hands. Finally, it is critical that you keep your feet dry and clean as often as possible when it comes to living in the bush. Wear proper footgear, wash your feet regularly, dry them off completely, and keep them in clean socks and shoes as often as you possibly can. When you are navigating backwoods, your feet become exposed due to the constant walking, climbing, and navigating of rugged terrain. They can also become damp, dirty, and easily injured if you are not careful. An injured foot can quickly become infected due to ongoing exposure and use, which can lead to a dangerous and even deadly situation. Keeping your feet dry and clean is imperative at all times. If you do sustain an injury to your foot, practice maximum care in keeping it clean at all times to avoid an infection.

For camp hygiene, you want to boil and cleanse everything as soon as it is used, including camp cookware and any other tools you have been using around raw meat or other contaminants. Your clothes should be washed out as needed in a nearby stream and hung to dry in the sunlight. Whenever possible, hang things such as your bedding and worn clothes that are not quite ready to be washed yet in the sunlight. Sun kills bacteria within hours, so this is a great way to keep everything cleansed and neutralized.

Organization can be achieved in whatever way you want; however, you should have a clear system, and you should stick with that system. Keep all of your cookware in one clean spot. Keep all of your tools organized and easy to access. Keep your sleeping hut away from your eating space, and keep your firewood in an easy to access safe spot. Your food should be stored safely away from camp, yet in an easy to access spot so that if any animals do happen across it, they cannot find it, but they also cannot find you in the process.

As far as protection goes, there are many steps you can take to protect yourself. Sleeping with an axe, machete, or other similar weapons on hand is a good idea as this can help you protect yourself from any animals that may surprise you. Otherwise, never sleep in the clothes you cooked in; keep a source of light and bear spray on hand if you have any, and if you have any pets, keep them leashed and close by so they do not attract animals. Always sleep at least 100 yards away from where you store your food and do your cooking so you are not discovered if an animal discovers your food, and they will. Build your shelter in such a way that makes it challenging for anything else to get in there with you, and always keep a fire going at all hours of the day and night. Generally, fire and smoke from the fire will deter animals from bothering you. The fire you keep going near your sleep shelter should, naturally, be different from the fire you cook over.

CHAPTER 4

Building And Managing Fires

Fires are a primary tool when it comes to surviving in the woods. You are going to have at least two fires that you will need to create and maintain, though if you find yourself venturing away from camp for hunting or fishing, you may need to create additional, smaller fires on the go. Knowing how to build fires properly and safely is an essential skill for survival.

The Triangle of Fire

A fire can be started with three elements, and it can also be stopped by eliminating one of the three elements. The three elements required for fire include heat, fuel, and oxygen. In fire crafting, you want to intentionally create a safe space where you can add fuel, create heat, and maintain high oxygen levels so that your fire can thrive. You will do this by constructing a fire lay that allows ample oxygen to get in and around your fire, which allows you to place added wood (fuel) without smothering your fire, and to use the fire as needed without smothering it or hurting yourself in the process.

Anytime you build a fire in the woods, you should also be prepared to put that fire out. This way, if your fire gets out of control or needs to be eliminated for any reason, you can safely do so. The two best ways to stop a fire in the woods is to either drench it in water or smother it with dirt. Keeping a pail of water nearby can be useful to eliminate your fire, or you can shovel dirt onto it if it gets out of control to smother it.

Placing Your Fire

When you place a fire, you want to consider where the fire is going so that you can preserve the safety of your camp and maintain the benefit of the fire. Your food fire, as stated, should be kept at least 100 yards away from your sleeping arrangements. That way, if any food drippings fall into the fire or if it begins to accumulate a smell, animals will be attracted away from where you are, rather than toward where you are. Your fire for warmth, light, and protection should be built closer to your sleeping arrangements so that you can rely on it as needed. This fire should, however, be built a bit away from your sleeping arrangements so that it cannot accidentally catch your sleeping arrangements on fire and burn you in your sleep.

All fires should be built in such a way that they will be easy to contain, that they will not catch any nearby bushes and that they will not grow too high to catch the tree branches above. This way, you are not running the risk of creating a fire that is larger than you can reasonably control.

Fire Lays

The best fire lay that you can use in the woods is a teepee lay. If you are just creating a fire for warmth, you can construct a circle out of rocks on the ground and build a teepee fire inside of it. If you are looking to cook with your fire, you will want to make a smaller teepee so that your fire does not get too hot, and so that you can create a cooktop surface.

The Teepee Fire Lay

The teepee fire lay is created by taking several thick branches cut to about 2 feet long or less, depending on the height of the fire you want. Then, you will lean all of the branches up together in a cone shape, with the point toward the sky, like a teepee. You will then place kindling and fire-starting material in the center of the teepee so that you can light that part on fire. As the fire builds within the teepee, it will catch the branches on fire, effectively giving you a strong fire to keep yourself warm or to cook over.

Log Cabin Fires

A log cabin fire lay is made by taking various branches and pieces of wood that are no more than 1" thick, as this will make it easier for all of them to catch fire. You may want the wood bases to be slightly thicker though, around 1.5-2" thick so that it is more sturdy. You will then lay two sticks parallel to each other, and then run two perpendicular to them across the edges. You will go back and forth, crisscrossing your branches until they look like a pyramid. Then, you will build a similar structure around the edges of this by crisscrossing wood; only this time, you will not form them into a pyramid shape but rather keep them square. These sticks should be somewhat thicker, around 2-3" or up to 4" at the base. You won't need to build your fire too tall, maybe 4-6 levels. Then, you will light the small inner pyramid on fire and let it get going. It will then catch the larger log cabin formation outside of it on fire, giving you a nice, healthy fire to work with.

Long Log Fires

A long log fire is used if you need your fire to burn all night. This is important, especially if you are in a cooler climate or somewhere where you will need access to ongoing warmth and light. You will make your long log fire by digging a shallow depression into the ground, about 6' long and 1' wide. Then, you will build a fire that fills the length of the depression using a log cabin formation but spreading it the length of the depression. Once the fire is going, you should find that it burns down into the ground creating good hot coals and a nice roaring fire. You will then put two long logs on top of the fire, running the length of the depression. This should keep your fire running all night long.

Dakota Fire Pits

Dakota fire pits are a type of fire that is nestled into a hole that you dig into the ground. They are easily contained, provide great heat, function excellent in high wind areas, and they can help you remain stealthy if need be. A Dakota fire hole needs to be built anywhere where there is a flat surface that you can easily dig into, but where the ground is hard enough that it won't collapse when dug into. Once you have decided on your location, you need to completely clear away any vegetation from where you are going to place the fire. Then, you are going to dig a hole. A hole that is deeper will be less visible from the surface, while a hole that is wider will make a bigger fire. Pick what you need most. After you have dug out your main hole, you will need to dig a second hole on an angle, connecting into the bottom of the main hole. Do not connect the hole with your shovel, but instead dig in and connect the hole with your hand; this way, you do not accidentally collapse the earth around it. The hole should be about the size of your fist, as this is going to feed oxygen to your fire so that your fire can continue to burn. Once you have set the pit, you should start a fire in the hole using dry brush and other starting materials. Then, you can start to add larger sticks until your fire is burning consistently. Your fire is ready to go!

The Cooking Fire Lay

A simple cooking fire lay, also called a bundle fire is created by taking logs that are all about the same height and bundling them together with the cut sides both up and down, creating a flat surface on the top of them. You will hold the bundle up using bindings and rocks on either side. Then, you will light a fire under the bundle using a fire starter. As the fire begins to lick the top of your surface, you can place your pot or pan on top of the fire and cook. Note that you want to cook before the logs get too burnt as they will start to fall and could cause a dangerous situation if your pot falls into the fire and splashes water or hot food anywhere.

Starting Materials

There are many starting materials you can use when it comes to getting a fire going. If you are able to bring starting materials with you, bring cardboard, cotton swabs, dryer lint, and citrus peels or nutshells with you as these are all great fire starters. If you need to find fire-starting materials in the wild, look for pine cones, pine needles, cattails, cedar chips from splitting wood, dried grass, moss, and even small dried twigs and leaves as these are all great for starting a fire with. Avoid putting anything damp in there, such as moss or damp brush from the bottom of the forest, as these will dampen your fire and prevent any proper fire from starting.

Sourcing Wood

Sourcing wood in the woods is easy, though picking the right tree is important. There are a few things you need to consider when it comes to picking your tree. First, you want to start by looking for trees that have already died and fallen over, as they will be dry and ready to burn. If you must cut down a live tree, you will need to wait several days for it to properly dry out so that it can be burnt. Otherwise, you need to slowly add them to your fire so that the fire can dry them out first, before catching them on fire. If you must pick a live tree, pick a tree or a large branch that is not too thick so that it will dry out faster. You also want to make sure the tree is far enough away from camp that you do not risk damaging your camp if it falls over, but close enough to camp that you can haul it back.

If you are chopping back a live tree, you will cut a notch in the side facing the direction you want it to fall in. Note that it will not always fall this way, so you will still need to be careful to watch where it is going. You can create the notch by cutting into the tree at a 45-degree angle up and down so that there is a complete notch cut into the side. This notch should go no more than ¼ to 1/3 of the way into the tree to avoid making the notch so big that the tree falls while you are still cutting it. Once you have cut in your notch, you will go to the opposite side of the tree and cut straight into it. Ideally, as soon as the tree is cut through, it will fall toward the notch. You can increase this likelihood by avoiding trees that have obviously heavy branches on the side opposite of where you want it to fall, and by avoiding cutting trees on heavy wind days, especially when the wind is not blowing in a favorable direction.

After you have cut the tree, you will chop it into manageable sized logs on the spot then drag those logs back to camp. There, you can process them by cutting them down into smaller logs that are fit for burning in your fires. You should keep your log reserve full at all times to ensure that you always have fuel for your fires.

CHAPTER 5

Navigation And Tracking

Perhaps one of the scariest, yet most important skills that you need to know about when it comes to bushcrafting is navigation and tracking. Knowing how to navigate the terrain you are in, keeping track of yourself, and tracking necessary survival resources is important if you are going to survive. With that being said, it can be incredibly simple to get turned around backward in the woods and to find yourself confused with where you are, where you are going, and where you need to be. Proper navigation and tracking skills will keep you clear on where you are and easily able to navigate the terrain you are living in.

The trick with navigation is to realize that when you are stressed out and scared, it can be incredibly easy for you to forget everything and find yourself completely confused and lost. A startling sound, feeling a little too hungry, thirsty, or tired, or even an encounter with wildlife can throw you off course and have you wondering how to get back on track. For that reason, it is important that you educate yourself on navigation and tracking, practice it as often as you can, and do your best to be as meticulous as possible with navigation and tracking should you ever find yourself in a survival situation. This way, you are unlikely to find yourself permanently lost and at-risk due to exposure and a lack of protection in the woods.

Using Your Compass Properly

Knowing how to use a compass properly can seem somewhat intimidating if you have never had to do it before. Fortunately, using a compass is relatively easy and can be learned quickly. The first thing you need to know before using a compass is the different parts of the compass and what they do. Your compass has seven different parts that aid you in navigation: the baseplate, the direction of travel arrow, the compass housing, the degree dial, the magnetic needle, the orienting arrow, and the orienting lines.

The baseplate and compass housing are both parts of the casing for the compass. The baseplate is a plastic plate where the compass is embedded, where the compass housing is the plastic shell that houses the magnetized needle inside of the compass itself.

The direction of travel arrow is the arrow inside of the baseplate that points away from the arrow. The degree dial is a dial that can be twisted to display all 360 degrees of a circle. The magnetic needle points north and south. The orienting arrow is a non-magnetic arrow inside of the compass housing, and the orienting lines run parallel to the orienting arrow.

To use your compass, you will start by holding it in your flat palm and gently rotating it side to side to ensure that your magnetic arrow is properly functioning. This ensures the compass gets an accurate read, and that it is working properly. Next, you want to figure out what direction you are facing. To do this, you will turn the degree dial until the orienting arrow lines up with the north end of the magnetic arrow. Once the arrows are lined up, look at the direction of travel arrow on the baseplate, which will indicate what direction you are going. If it falls between E and S, for example, you are facing southeast.

As you look at your arrow, you will need to tell the difference between "true" north and "magnetic" north. True north refers to the point where all longitudinal lines meet up at the top of the map, also known as the north pole. Magnetic north is the tilt of the magnetic field, which is about eleven degrees different from the tilt of the earth's axis. The difference between these two measures is called "declination." This difference can cause up to 20 degrees of difference between magnetic north and true north in different terrains. You will have to account for the shift to get a truly accurate reading of your map. Note that traveling even just one degree off from what your map says can lead to you being 100 feet or 30 meters off track, which can be a major difference when traveling in the backwoods.

Correcting the declination or difference between true north and magnetic north requires you to know where the line of zero is in your area. The best way to do this is to research it ahead of time and to research the line of zero for where you are likely to find yourself in a state of survival. This way, you can be sure that you have true north. This will matter most when you find yourself following someone else's map, as any official map will be made using true north, not magnetic north for that area.

When you are ready to begin traveling, you need to start by finding your bearings. Twist the dial until the orienting arrow, and the north end of the magnetic arrow is aligned, then pay attention to where you are now. If you have a true map you are following, adjust your dial for the declination in your area. Next, you need to identify the exact direction you need to be going, and then you need to hold your compass up to help ensure that you are walking in that direction the entire time. If you are unable to hold your compass up for extended periods of time, you can do what is called "leapfrogging." Leapfrogging means that you identify your intended direction, identify an object in the distance that exactly aligns with that direction, and walk there until you reach that location. Then, you take out your compass and check for your next directional point. Keep doing this until you get where you need to go.

When you have a map that has already been created, either by you or someone else, you can use that map to help you find your direction of travel and to help you find your bearings. To do this, place your map on a horizontal surface and lay your compass over the directional arrow points on the map so you can identify true north. Then, slide your compass until it's edge crosses over your current location with the orienting arrow still pointing north. Draw a line along the edge at your current position. Taking your bearing from the map this way will require you to then identify the exact point where you want to end up. Next, use the edge of your compass to create a line between where you are and where you want to go. Now, rotate your degree dial so that the orienting arrow points toward true north, and identify exactly what direction you need to head in order to get where you are going based on the direction of your compass. Simply follow that direction until you reach your intended point, as this will give you a new bearing to help you navigate your terrain with.

Following a Map

Ideally, you want to gather a printed map (or two) of the location you will be living in so that you know exactly where everything is. This will make locating a campsite, discovering water, and learning the terrain much faster. You can often find specific survival maps online for the location where you expect you will be surviving in when you leave an urban environment. When it comes to following a map, especially a detailed map of the environment you are in, there are a few things you need to know to help you follow that map.

Topographic maps, or maps of back wood locations, will have details that allow you to know what type of terrain is being represented on the map, and what distances are being represented on the map. The scale will generally be shown in miles and will show you how much of the map represents a certain amount of miles. For example, one inch on the map may represent 2 miles in real life. If your terrain has mountains in it, there will be another scale that shows you how to identify the heights of those mountains. Mountains are represented by round lines that encompass the entirety of the mountain itself, and every fifth line is thicker and has an actual number identifying the height of that part of the terrain. If the circles represented on your map are notched all the way around, this means you are looking at a depression or a valley, rather than a mountain.

Other terrains, including peaks, ridgelines, cliffs, peaks, valleys, saddles, places with sparse vegetation, and spaces with dense vegetation, will also be visible on your map. Each map will come with a legend that lets you know what each color means and what each symbol on the map means, effectively helping you determine what the terrain around you looks like.

Maps have five colors on them, including brown, green, blue, black, and red. Brown represents contour lines, which indicate elevation. Green represents vegetation. Blue represents water sources. Black represents man-made objects or structures. Red represents major roadways. White represents "nothing." For example, if you see a white space with some green splashed within it, this means the area has sparse vegetation, and nothing significant around it, as well as no significant inclination or sloping.

When you are traveling long distances, you will want to identify the different points where you will be passing through as you travel so that you can create milestones in your path. This way, you can aim toward each milestone and practice leapfrogging to help you get there. Then, you can pull out your map and find your next location to head toward. In due time, you will find yourself exactly where you need to be.

The Five Navigation Methods You Need

As you travel, there are five navigation methods that will help you feel confident that you are exactly where you need to be, and that you are safe. These methods will also help you maintain your bearings and successfully navigate your way to your destination. They include handrails, backstops, baselines, aiming off, and panic azimuths.

Handrails are a form of navigation method whereby you use a certain feature or item to create a guide that takes you where you want to go. Once you navigate your way to a handrail, you simply need to follow it, and you can trust that it will take you where you need to go. Handrails can either be a certain element on your map, or they can be something you create yourself. For example, if you are in an area that has a body of water, you may use a certain length of the body of water as a handrail to guide you toward where you are going. As long as you stay near the water for that amount of time, you know you are where you need to be. You will also easily be able to find yourself again. Making your own handrail can be done by having a particular marker that you use to track out a certain trail or area where you will be heading to frequently, such as a popular place for hanging snares or the area where you will be cooking your food. You can make your own markers by marking trees or branches with certain marks, by tying something around multiple trees or branches along the way, or by otherwise marking your trail. This way, you know exactly where to go every single time.

Backstops are landmarks you hit that you will not cross at any given time. They are important as they prevent you from traveling too far. If you hit a backstop, you know you need to stop and turn around. You should define backstops on all four sides of your camping area, and define backstops anytime you are leaving camp to go somewhere. Even if you are not intending on going far, backstops will help.

Baselines are geographic boundaries that are designed to keep you in certain areas. While your backstop is designed to prevent you from traveling out of bounds, your baseline can help you identify where you are and how to get where you are going. A great example of a baseline would be a main road or a major trail traveling along the length of your camp. These would be fairly easy to stumble across and, once you were on them, you would have a good idea of where you are and where you need to go from there to get back to where you need to be.

Aiming off is a method that allows you to deliberately set yourself on a course that is off to one side of your destination. For example, let's say where you need to go is exactly northwest of where you are, you would purposefully go a little further north. The reason for aiming off is that it allows you to get exactly where you need to go every single time by knowing exactly where your destination is from where you have arrived. Let's say that you are going out to set traps, and there is a cliff as a backstop for your trip. If you tried to aim directly for where you have set your traps, you might be a few degrees off and then miss your traps. At this point, you would know whether to go left or right because you would not know whether you had gone a little too far to the right or to the left when you were traveling to find your traps. If, however, you had purposefully aimed off to the right, you would know that no matter how off you may have been, all you have to do is turn left and walk along the cliff to find your traps. Purposefully aiming off a little to the wrong direction ensures that once you reach that destination, you know exactly which way to go to get to your actual destination, and it is a lot easier to get there because now you are much closer. In other words, it makes it easier for you to keep your bearings.

Panic azimuths are basically backup plans when you are traveling, and they are the easiest way to find yourself when you are lost. A panic azimuth should be planned out before you leave, and it should be used anytime you find yourself either lost or dealing with a problem that requires you to abort your mission in the bush. Essentially, you are going to pick a specific direction that you will walk in order to help yourself become found again. For example, let's say your cooking camp is 100 yards southeast of your sleeping camp. Perhaps you set off to get there but were a few degrees off and so now you cannot find your cooking camp. At this point, you would either decide to go only south or only east until you reach a familiar landmark that helps you find yourself. Pick one based on what is easiest in your terrain. For example, if south of your cooking area, there is a nearby body of water, then only go south until you reach that body of water. At that point, you will have a general idea as to where you are and how to get back to camp from there.

Determining Distance When Traveling

Maps always define how to get somewhere based on the number of miles or number of kilometers traveled. When you have an actual navigation system on you, it is easy to identify how far you have traveled. However, in the backwoods, digital navigation systems are unavailable, so you are going to need to know how to measure how far you have traveled to ensure that you do not go too far, or not reach quite far enough. Pedometers, or step counters, are a great way to keep track of yourself in the bush. With a pedometer, the device counts the number of steps you take. You should make sure your pedometer is well calibrated in advance to avoid having an ill calibrated pedometer throwing you off course. It takes roughly 2,000 steps for an adult to walk one mile, so you will need to calculate your course based on that. For example, if you know you need to go 1.5 miles east before turning south, you will need to go roughly 3,000 steps east before turning south. Be sure to keep track of your pedometer to avoid getting lost.

Finding Yourself When You're Lost

Panic azimuths are the fastest and easiest way to find yourself when you are lost in a bush. If, however, you find yourself still lost, there are two options you can take to help you find yourself. The first option is to climb to the highest ground you can reach and look around to see where you are. This should help you get an idea of where you need to go in order to find yourself. The other option is to follow the land or keep walking until you find a body of water and then follow the body of water until you reach someplace familiar. If you do not seem to find your way back to camp or civilization, be sure to look out for evidence of human existence. A trailblazer, tire tracks, previous campfires, and other such things are great evidence that humans have been around, and if you follow these signs, you should be able to find your way out in no time. Finally, you can use the sun as a compass if you need to. The sun rises in the east and sets in the west, so as long as you know whether it is morning or afternoon, you can use the sun to help guide you. If it is morning, the sun will be in the eastern sky, while if it is afternoon, it will be in the western sky. If it is dead ahead, this means it is noon. Wait about an hour or so, and the sun will move toward the west, and you will be able to use it to guide your way back to camp again.

CHAPTER 6

Securing And Storing Food And Water

After you have secured shelter and fire, which will protect your core temperature, you need to start focusing on securing yourself food and water. Water should count as your first order of business, as you can only live for 3 days without water, whereas you can live for up to 3 weeks without food. With that being said, the longer you go without either, the weaker you will become, and the harder it will be for you to get any.

If you arrive at your campsite in the late afternoon, your only order of business should be to secure some water. If you arrive in the evening or later, you should wait until morning and do with whatever you have in your pack until then. You will last one night, even if you are beginning to feel uncomfortable. As soon as morning comes, you should fetch yourself some water and then prepare to get yourself some food. Even if you were able to bring food along with you and you are able to eat a decent breakfast, you should be on the hunt for food from day one. It can take a bit to get the hang of catching game, even if you have done it in the past, as you will have to be able to track the animals and set traps to catch them. That can take time. The sooner you get started, the sooner you will have a steady supply of food to keep you going.

Purifying and Storing Water

If you were able to prepare properly for a survival setting, you should have a bottle or a water filter that allows you to filter water right out of the water source. With that being said, even after the water has been filtered, you should still boil it to sterilize it from any potential bacteria that may have gotten through. It is always better to air on the side of caution, as water can contain harmful bacteria and parasites that can be dangerous to your health.

If you do not have a filter on hand, you can make a natural one using things you find in nature, as well as a shirt or a large piece of fabric. You will create your filter by placing your fabric over the top of a pot so that it caves in, somewhat like a bowl. Fix it in place, so it doesn't move. Then, you will add charcoal from the fire pit, dirt, sand, grass, and gravel on top of it. Next, you will pour your water through the homemade filter until it reaches the pot. Then, you will boil it to eliminate any further contaminants. While this is not the ideal solution, it will give you the best chance of being able to purify your water so that you are far less likely to fall ill from drinking it. You should keep your canteens full at all times, so you will likely need to fetch, filter, and boil water every day or every other day. Always do it before you completely run out, as you will want the boiling water to have plenty of time to cool down before you consume it. As well, make sure you cover the boiled water properly to avoid having any contaminants falling in after you have already cleaned it out.

Preparing to Trap Animals

Protein is essential in the bush, as you are using large amounts of energy. Protein is a slower burning fuel, so to speak, making it perfect for the type of energy you need for survival. You can source protein using traps. Trapping animals in the bush is the easiest way to source animals when you are without typical hunting tools like guns, bows, and arrows. If you do happen to have any of the latter on hand, though, you could use them to harvest larger mammals. With that being said, larger mammals are not ideal in the bush as you end up with more meat than you can reasonably eat or store, and that becomes a large threat as you are more likely to attract hungry animals who could attack you in the process of trying to steal your meat. If you do manage to ward off animals, you are still at risk of the meat spoiling before you can consume it all. And, lastly, you want to save your munitions for protection, just in case an animal comes up, and you are unable to reasonably escape or protect yourself without your weapons.

Trapping animals is relatively simple. All you need is an idea of where animals tend to spend most of their time, bait, and a properly made and set trap to help you capture the animals. Below, you will find everything you need to locate animals and trap them safely and as humanely as possible.

Signs for Finding Game

Animal signs are the key to successful trapping as these indicate that there are clearly animals present to be trapped. It can take some practice to find animal signs, as animals are rather good at hiding their tracks to avoid being hunted by other wildlife. Even so, you can still find them if you pay close attention. The signs of an animal being present include scat, fur, burrows, sounds, hordes of food, runways or rub marks, and animal tracks or claw marks.

Scat is often found along an animal's typical trail since wild animals are not known for seeking out specific areas to go to the bathroom. Fresh animal droppings will be shiny and soft, while any scat that has been out for a while will be dry and crumbly. You can identify the animal based on the size and shape. When you are trapping animals for food, you will want to find animals with scat that is relatively small, as this will indicate that you are following the track of a rabbit, a hare, or something of similar size and shape.

Fur is something that is commonly found in spring and fall, as animals tend to shed and grow new coats around this time of year. Even so, animals will shed mildly throughout most of the year, so you may find tufts of fur scattered around the area when you are tracking an animal. If you see fur in the area, it is a good sign that an animal has been present.

Burrows are good to look for, particularly when you are hunting for survival as they indicate the presence of a small or medium animal being present. You can also look for nests if you are looking to trap birds, as these indicate that birds are around. Note, however, that nests may be abandoned outside of breeding season in the spring and early summer, so nests alone may not be a strong enough indicator that birds are actively present.

Runways and rub marks are a good indicator that animals are present. Runways are trails that have been used so frequently that they are well worn in by the animal that is using them. If you were to follow a runway long enough, it is likely that you would eventually come across an animal or, at the very least, their home. Rub marks are from animals rubbing against things like trees, branches, or bushes. Larger mammals like deer, moose, bear, and other similar animals will leave rub marks from their antlers or claws higher up on trees. Be sure to watch for these, as moose and bear, in particular, can be very dangerous to come across so you will want to avoid being in these areas too much without some form of protection.

If you sit still and quiet long enough, you may begin to hear animals nearby, or even spot one if you are lucky. Sounds and spotting animals are surefire ways of knowing that an animal is, without a doubt, present.

Bait for Trapping

The type of bait you will use for animal traps depends on what type of animal you are targeting. For many rodents, their primary food source is either vegetation, or smaller meat sources. Leaving a small bite of fresh meat may seem like a great way to bait your trap. However, you are far more likely to attract larger animals with the scent, too, which can destroy your trap and possibly invite larger predators into the area, which will then compete for your food. Instead of using meat, find fresh berries, nuts, seeds, and other foraging foods and place them in a small pile like a buffet near your trap. This will encourage rodents to come without alerting larger predators to the idea of food being in the area.

The Components of a Trap

Every trap needs an anchor that will keep it in place, and an element that will actually trap the animal. The most simple traps to set are snares, and they are made by having snare wire, a slip knot, and a place to secure your snare so that an animal is not able to take off after getting caught. Another thing you need to be aware of is something that you yourself may not be able to detect, but that the animal you are attempting to trap will. That is, your scent. Unlike humans, animals have an additional capacity to smell heavy moisture-borne molecules and pheromones. Washing your hands or rubbing your hands on your body or each other before touching your trap can contaminate it with your small. Likewise, touching the trap too much can do the same. You want to minimize your contact with the snare and, if possible, wear gloves to prevent yourself from touching it. As well, do not wash your hands before you create and set snares, instead let them, and yourself, develop a natural odor first. This way, you are less likely to warn an animal that a trap is present. Finally, as one last word of caution, never, ever touch the noose part of a trap after it has been set. A properly set trap *will* seal, quickly, and cut severely cut you or even cut one of your digits off. Both of these are not ideal as they can pose an even higher threat in the wild as they already would in normal, everyday life.

Grave's Bait Triggered Snare

A graves bait triggered snare is the easiest snare to set, and it encourages animals to come into the snare itself, making you more likely to be able to trap animals this way. Building a grave's bait triggered snare requires you to have a spring pole, a forked stake, a pencil-diameter toggle stick, a snare line with an attached trigger line, a bait stick, and bait.

To set one, you will tie a snare line to the end of a spring pole, which is a long tree branch that can easily be bent without breaking. You can find a spring pole fresh off of any tree, as long as they are fairly thin and fresh they should bend easily. You will want to have one end of the pole firmly planted in the ground where it will stay put. Then, you will bend the other end of the spring pole over until it touches the ground, then mark that spot. Next, you will drive the forked stake into the ground in that exact spot, which will be used to keep the snare nice and open so that an animal will easily fit through it. If your snare collapses at all, it will be unlikely to catch anything. Next, you are going to tie your toggle to the end of the trigger line on your trap. Then, you will run the toggle under the fork on the stake, keeping it parallel to the ground and at a right angle to the stake. Your baited trigger stick should be set at the end of the toggle, which will set the trap. Now, you just need to go away and wait for it to trap something!

Fixed Snare

Fixed loop snares are made from solid wires or braided steel cables which offer strength, flexibility, and rigidity. These traps can only be used once, as once the animal has been taught, they will typically destroy the snare from kicking and attempting to break free. Aside from this fact, these snares are the fastest and easiest to create and set.

You will set your snare using a twig that is around 1/8" to 3/16" diameter. It should be breakable. You will wind one end of your wire around the twig three times then twist the twig in circles, causing the wire to twist closed. Next, you will break the twig off, which will reveal a circle left behind. Feed the other end of the wire through that circle, and you are left with a noose. These snares work best over burrows or runways, though they can also be used on spring poles to catch game.

Drowning Snare

A drowning snare is simple and can help you quickly put any animal out of its misery, often much faster than any of the other traps will. To successfully set a drowning snare, you will require a heavy rock, a stick that floats, a snare line with a noose made into it, and a stick to prop up the rock.

You will want to find a steep-banked waterway that animals frequently use to access water. Then, tie the snare line to the rock, leaving a length of snare line available for you to tie to a float stick. Next, you will set the nose in a runway or slide that heads straight to the water, and you will prop the rock up so that it will fall (easily) once the snare is activated. The minute the snare is activated, the rock should fall into the water, dragging the animal in behind it and drowning them. The float stick will show you where the animal is so that you can quickly grab it. This type of trap is great in cold water conditions as it preserves the animal and keeps it safe from scavengers.

Squirrel Pole Snare

A squirrel pole snare can be set using a 4' to 6' pole that is around the diameter of your arm. You will cover it in fixed snares and then prop it against a tree that has signs of squirrels frequenting that tree. Squirrels love shortcuts, so one will be likely to run up or down the pole, effectively catching themselves in the snare. Be sure to set several snares on one pole to maximize your chances of catching one.

Paiute Deadfall

A Paiute deadfall is set with the intention of delivering a killing blow to the back of a small mammals head with thanks to a fairly large rock. These traps were originally made by Native American hunters and trappers, and they work incredibly well. To hunt a prairie dog or a rat, you will need an 8" long "Y" shaped stick. You will also need a straight stick that is 9" and a bit thicker than a pencil, and a 2" stick that is thinner than a pencil. A slender bait stick will be needed, too. The bait stick should be about 12" and half the diameter of a pencil. Lastly, you will need about 8" of string, bait, and a flat rock that is around 5-10 pounds.

You will start by taking the 9" straight stick and tying a string to one end of it. Then, you will tie the other end around the 2" toggle. You will want to either wipe or skewer the bait on one end of the 12" bait stick. Now, you are going to stand the "Y" shaped stick up by the edge of the rock, with the "Y" part upright. The end of the 9" stick that does not have a string attached should be placed in the fork of the "Y" shaped stick, with only 1" of it toward the rock itself. Now, you are going to lift the edge of the rock up and prop it on the 1" piece of the 9" stick. Now, you are going to wrap the toggle halfway around the post, doing a 180-degree turn. You should be able to hold the rock up by the toggle itself, without actually having to hold the rock in place. Now, you're going to place the baited end of the 12" bait stick between the bottom of the stone and the toggle. As soon as the animal taps the 12" bait stick, the toggle will release, and the rock will drop on them, effectively delivering a killing blow.

Making a Small Trapping Kit for Your Pack

Having a trapping kit on hand when you are going into the bush at any time is important, as you never know when you may need to trap an animal. With that being said, you should educate yourself on trapping laws in your area beforehand, as certain areas have rendered trapping, or certain varieties of trapping, illegal.

Creating a trapping kit requires just three easy steps, and it can be kept in your pack or in your survival jacket whenever you are away from camp. Having a trapping kit ensures that you have everything you need to set traps, which will protect you in a survival setting. The first step to making a trapping kit is to add your snares. Keep braided steel cable, cord, and wire in your trapping kit so that you have everything you need for trapping. Ideally, you should keep an assortment of thicknesses and lengths so that you can trap anything at any size that you may need to in the bush.

Next, you are going to need some bait. MRE pouches of peanut butter last years in a survival kit and work perfectly for luring small animals such as rodents in your traps. A small tin of sardines can be useful, too, as you can rub a bait stick in the sardines and place it in your snare.

Lastly, you need something to help you eliminate your scent from the trap as animals will smell you and avoid your trap altogether if they catch your scent. De-scenting spray can be found in most hunting and fishing stores, and they work to help eliminate the scent off of traps. Powdered charcoal works, too, as you can rub your hands in it and then set your traps, as charcoal will absorb odors and cover your scent. Finally, an unscented trash bag or other similar things could be used as they will provide a complete barrier between your hands and the trap.

Fishing With Improvised Rods

If you find yourself having to fish when you are in the wild, the best way to do so is through making an improvised rod. Taking a simple stick about two or three finger widths wide and around 4' to 5' long will work perfectly. You will want to keep it relatively short and thick, as this ensures that the end will not snap off in the process. You can then attach a fishing line to the end of the stick, and attach a small hook with bait on the other end. A worm or a small bug works perfectly when baiting fish.

You will want to find an area where fish tend to congregate. Pools of water next to larger moving bodies of water are great, as they tend to accumulate a large amount of fish who are taking a rest from swimming. Go in the early morning or later day, as this is when you are likely to find the most fish gathered. Then, drop your line in and flick it above the surface of the water a few times to garner interest. Let it hang for a few seconds before doing it again. If nothing happens, let the line sink into the water a little bit and drag it around to make your bait act like a real bug. This will do wonders in attracting the attention of fish.

CHAPTER 7
Processing Game Meat

Once you have caught an animal to eat, you are going to need to know how to process it so that you can safely consume it. Processing game meat properly is imperative, as it allows you to achieve two things. First, properly processing your meat prevents you from damaging the meat before you even get a chance to eat it. Organs such as the stomach, the bladder, and the anus contain substances that will destroy the meat. Anything that comes out of the inside of the stomach, bladder, or anus will contaminate the meat to the point where it is no longer safely consumable by humans. You must be cautious when processing meat to avoid damaging the organs and destroying your meat in the process. Secondly, you need to process it properly so that you can cook it thoroughly to avoid catching any bacteria, viruses, or parasites that an animal may have had. You also need to practice regular, every-day hygiene when processing and eating game by washing your hands thoroughly and keeping yourself clean so that you do not spread bacteria, viruses, or parasites through contaminated hands or cookware.

Small Mammals

Small mammals like rats, prairie dogs, and squirrels all need to be butchered carefully as they are well-known for carrying highly infectious diseases. Squirrels, for example, still carry the black plague even though it has been eradicated from humans. Exercising caution when preparing these animals ensures that they are properly prepared for eating and that they are able to be cooked thoroughly to avoid falling ill from consuming their meat.

The first step in processing small mammals is to make a small incision in the belly of the animal. Take care just to cut through the skin, and not through the meat itself, to avoid puncturing the organs. Next, you will make a cut all the way around the torso, just under the skin. Again, you do not want to cut the meat; you are just cutting through the skin. Now, you are going to work your fingers under the skin on the side where the backbone is, and then you will pull the skin off, pulling the top half over the head and the bottom half over the bottom of the animal. All the meat should still be intact at this point. Now, you will cut the back legs, neck, and tail, then remove them all from the animal.

Now, you will use your game shears to cut into the anus, up through the pelvis, and all the way into the neck. With two fingers, you will open the cut you have made and grab the heart, lungs, and esophagus. Pull them gently yet firmly down toward the tail, which will cause them all to easily fall out of the body cavity, leaving you with a clean inner cavity. Lastly, you will rinse the animal and place it in a bag or a bucket to carry it back to camp with you.

Medium Mammals

Medium size mammals are a little easier to butcher because they are larger, which means they're not quite as finicky. You will still need to be careful with your blade to avoid destroying your meat. With that being said, you will receive more cuts from your meat because there is more meat to cut in the first place. While small mammals like rodents are generally kept as one single piece of meat, medium mammals will be cut into different portions, creating multiple pieces of meat to be cooked and consumed.

The following explanation for how to butcher a medium mammal will be written for a hare specifically, but it can be used on any medium mammal such as a bobcat, a fox, an otter, or any other similarly sized animal.

You will start by making something for you to hang the animal from. In the bush, you could simply tie two lengths of rope tightly around the back legs of the mammal and then hang them from a low hanging branch where it is easy for you to reach the entirety of the animal for processing it.

Once the animal is hung, you will place a bucket under it and then use game shears to cut off the head and the two front feet. Wait until the animal completely bleeds out into the bucket below before moving on to the next step. Once your animal has completely bled out, you will make two incisions around the ankles on the back legs. These incisions should only go deep enough to cut into the pelt, but not the meat, and should completely detach the leg skin from the foot skin. Facing the back of the animal, or where the animal's spine is, you will take your knife and cut another incision from the inner part of the incision on the ankle down above the tail, leaving the tail and the anus intact. You will now do this again on the other leg. There should be a "V" shaped tuft of fur remaining over the tail. Go around to the stomach side of the animal and do the same thing, cutting a "V" shape out around the genitalia. Now, because you have clipped off the front feet and head, you should be able to use your hands to firmly, yet gently tug the entire pelt right off the animal, pulling down toward the ground. If you will be surviving for a while, you will want to cut down either side of the pelt so that you have two pelts: one side from the stomach, and one side from the back. Then, you will hang it taut between several branches, away from where any animals could reach it, to help it dry out. These can be used to help warm up a cold tent, to insulate your clothes and keep you warm, or for any other number of purposes in a survival camp.

With the pelt off the animal, you will now cut the two front legs off and put them in your "keep" bucket, not the blood bucket. You will need to use a sharp knife to hack through the joint, as

70

you will not necessarily be cutting through the bones but rather breaking them apart so that you can rip the leg off while simultaneously cutting the meat from the shoulder so that you end up with two leg pieces.

Now, you will go to the backside of the animal and run your blade down one length of the spine, cutting as deep as the ribs. Then, you will do it again on the other side. When you insert your hand here and pull the meat away from the backbone, you should see spaces where you can cut the meat away from the animal altogether. Make those cuts and place those in your keep bucket with the front legs and any organs you may have harvested.

Next, from the stomach side of the animal, you will make a small 1" incision in the stomach of the animal. Then, you will insert your hands into the stomach incision and gently press the organs back and pull the skin forward. Very carefully cut the skin all the way down to the clavicle or the shoulder bone. Be careful not to damage any of the organs in the process, or else the meat will become useless. Once the stomach has been opened, carefully use your hand to pull all of the organs outside of the incision. You may want to harvest the heart, kidneys, and liver to consume as organ meat. However, it is not necessary. Do be aware that more parasites will be likely to live inside of organ meats, so if you choose to consume them, they will need to be cooked until they are well-done to thoroughly kill off any bacteria, viruses, or parasites.

Lastly, you want to cut off the two back legs of the animal by cutting close to the tail and straight down, and then over. Again, you will need to use the knife to help dislodge the joint and cut the meat at the same time. The backbone, tail, and bone pieces of the animal can then be discarded, and the legs can be kept. Rinse the meat off and then cook it!

If you are in a serious survival situation, bones from medium mammals can be used as tools. So, you may want to take the entire carcass back to camp and boil the skeleton until the meat is falling off. Then, remove the skeleton from the water, and when it is cool enough, pull all of the meat off. You will want to boil the clean bones one more time to neutralize any bacteria. Store them somewhere where you can easily access them. They can be turned into toggles, used to stake things down, sharpened to help spear fish out of the water, and even carved into sewing needles in a pinch.

Birds

Harvesting birds is entirely different from mammals because you have to remove the feathers. While pelts can be removed easily and usually in one fell swoop, feathers must be removed one at a time. The easiest way to pluck a bird is to start by cutting the wing of the bird off at the "elbow" joint in the wing, or the joint further down from the shoulder. This part of the wing is not meaty and is therefore not worth keeping.

Next, you will boil a large pot of water that is big enough for you to completely dunk the bird into the water. Then, holding the feet, you will dunk the bird in the water and hold it there for one and a half minutes. It is important to submerge the bird using oven-safe mitts and to pull it back out using tongs, as you do not want to burn yourself on hot water or steam. Once the minute and a half has gone by, you will pull the bird back out and lay it on a flat surface. Then, you will remove the feathers from the tail up to the head. They should easily fall right out at this point.

Now, you are going to cut through the skin at the point of the breast bone and cut straight along the center of the breastbone toward the center of the legs. You can pull the two pieces of skin outward, away from each other, so that they tug right off the meat. If they are stubborn, use your knife to separate the skin from the meat.

Flip the bird over onto its stomach and fold the wings all the way out and up. Cut behind each shoulder blade down to the bottom of the wing, and then cut off the feet. With birds, you will want to make a few incisions around the knee joint and then bend it back and forth until it breaks off. Now, you're going to cut and pull the skin and fat off from around the legs and thighs.

Finally, you want to cut off the wings completely and remove the remaining skin. Then, you will cut off the bird's back legs running along the side of the bird and into the fold of the thigh and down toward the tail space. Then, you will make cuts between the body and throat, coming to a "V" shape from either side of the throat. This will allow you to pull the neck of the bird out and any inner organs out, too. Lastly, you will carefully make an incision down the back from the neck incision until you reach the gut pouch. Then, you will pull it out and rip it free. Immediately dispose of the gut tract. Rinse your bird and cook it up!

Fish

Fish are probably the easiest to process at camp. Once you catch one, you will use the side of your blade to descale the fish. Run the side of your blade across the fish, dragging it side to side and always pulling away from the blade itself, until all of the scales have been removed. Then, remove the fins, the head all the way back to the gills, and the tail. Next, you will hold your knife horizontally and insert it into the fish by the tail end and carefully cut up about halfway through the fish and drag your blade toward the head, creating a horizontal incision along the length of the fishes belly. You will then carefully open the fish, reach in, and remove its entire innards. Wash the fish and prepare to cook it!

Reptiles and Amphibians

Reptiles and amphibians are common in some areas, and eating them is a good way of getting protein into your system. Reptiles and amphibians will differ in how they are processed based on whether or not they have legs. If they do have legs, but they are incredibly small, such as on a skink, you will more or less follow the same method for processing a reptile without legs, like a snake. You will simply cut the legs off as they are too small to eat anyway.

You will start to butcher an amphibian by cutting off all of its feet. Then, you will flip the amphibian over and use your game shears to cut through the skin of the amphibian. Start just above the thigh on one of the back legs and cut across the belly toward the other thigh. This part can be tough as amphibians tend to have very thick, tough skin, so be careful not to cut your hands in the process. With the incision started, go ahead and continue it around the back of the amphibian. Then, insert your fingers in through the incision and tug the skin off the rump and the top of the amphibian. Now, you will chop the legs off at the waist, keeping the two legs attached to each other. Then, you will chop one more time to separate the legs from the amphibian. While you could attempt to process the upper half of the amphibian, there will be a lot of organs in there, which makes it challenging and results in you not getting much meat out of it. So, just eat the legs. Be sure to rinse them and prepare them for cooking once you are done.

Snakes should be hung by the tail. Then, you should cut their heads off and give them time to bleed out. Then, you will use a sharp knife and make an incision on the belly part starting at the head and splitting the snake all the way back to the tail. Now, you will separate the skin from the meat, starting at the head side, and peel up toward where the snake has been tied. Discard the skin and use a pair of game shears and your hands to carefully remove and discard the innards. Now, cut off the tail end. Your snake is ready to be cooked.

Cooking Your Meat

Cooking meat in the bush always needs to be done properly to avoid making yourself sick. The easiest way to cook your meat is to cook it over a campfire like you are cooking over a stove. You can do this by putting your meat into one of your cooking pots or pans and cooking it until it is extremely well done all the way through. Ideally, you want to cook it until it is *more* done than you would at home since you will not have a meat thermometer handy to help you check for doneness. Further, many of the animals you may catch may not be able to be checked for doneness since they are not often standard to eat. It is likely that the outside of your meat will look charred and burnt, but that is exactly what you want, so long as your meat was cooked over fairly low temperatures. You can achieve the perfect temperature for cooking meat this way by cooking it over the embers of a low burning fire, which ensures that it is hot but not *too* hot.

Another way you can cook meat over the fire is by skewering it onto the end of a stick. Start by holding the stick in the heat near the fire for a few minutes to sterilize it. Then, skewer the meat onto the end of the stick and hold the meat down low into the edge of the base of the fire where the embers are burning it. Rotate it regularly and cook it until it is crispy and well-cooked all the way through. Again, look for charred edges and what would normally be considered "overcooked" to ensure that any possible contaminants are killed off, and you are safe to consume the meat.

Preserving Meat

Trapping more meat than you need for a single meal is a great way to make sure that you are able to have plenty to eat for a while, but then comes the question of how to preserve it. You need to be able to safely preserve *and* store your meat in a way where it will be cooked enough to keep you from getting sick and where it will not attract animals to your camp and put you in harms' way. Once you begin preserving meat, it is important that you know that you need to exercise extra caution when going back to the place where you have stored your meat to avoid being ambushed by a predator while you are trying to fetch your meat.

Drying

Before you can preserve your meat, you need to keep it cool, keep it clean and keep it dry. Let's say you have just caught something; you are going to want to process it and clean it in cool water as quickly as possible, which will help you keep that meat cool and ready to be cooked or preserved when the time comes. If you gather meat from your traps and it is particularly hot out, you should consider processing your meat near the trap so that you can get the pelt and guts separated. Then, you can clean the meat in a cool stream or in cool water. If it is particularly hot out, consider carrying two containers to move your meat in a smaller bucket, and a larger one. Fill the larger one with a bit of cool water, then place the smaller one inside of it and put your meat in there. This will weigh more to carry around, but it will also keep your meat cooler and prevent it from spoiling before you can either cook or preserve it.

If you are going to dry meat for preservation, the quickest way to do so is to use the sun as your tool. Slice your meat into thin strips, taking care not to leave any thick areas on the strips as thicker areas will take longer to dry and could develop harmful bacteria before try are dried. You also need to cut away any fat as it will not dry properly. Then, you need to cool, clean, and dry the surface of the meat using the aforementioned methods. Then, you will hang the meat high in a tree or from another structure that will be challenging for any wildlife to get it. The meat should be high enough above the ground that no one can stand up and reach it and low enough from the branch that no one can reach down from the top of the branch and get it. It should also be kept in the sunlight so that the sun can quickly dry everything out.

Drying your meat this way will keep your meat good for 1-2 months. With that being said, always tear a piece of meat in half, first, to ensure there is no moisture inside before you eat it.

Smoking

Smoking meat changes the surface of the meat to one that is more acidic, which will effectively kill off any bacteria in the meat and any bacteria that try to contaminate the meat. This works the same way that using smoke to cleanse yourself works. As well, the taste of smoked meat is quite delicious for many.

It is important to note that smoking is not the same as cooking. You are bathing the meat in smoke, not warming it up from the fire, and that dries it out and preserves it. It is important to choose a good hardwood when smoking your meat, such as hickory, cherry, maple, applewood, or oak. Softwoods like pine or spruce will have way too much resin in them, and they will damage the quality of flavor in your meat.

The best wood for smoking is dry wood or dead wood that has already fallen from the tree or been cut off and sitting to dry for weeks. Fresh cut wood will produce wet smoke, which will not work well in curing your meat.

To cure your meat with smoke, you will start by slicing it thin. Then, you will make a diamond shelter tarp lay, while using another tarp to cover the "entrance" into your tarp "hut." You want to build your diamond shelter tarp lay on top of a small hill, with the "entrance" facing down the hill rather than up. Then, you will dig a fire pit into the ground near the entrance of the tarp, but not at the entrance of the tarp, to avoid catching the tarp on fire. Next, you will light the fire and use rocks to block half of the fire that is away from the makeshift smokehouse so that the smoke can only blow toward the tarp. You will then prop the entrance of the tarp partially open where all of the smoke is billowing from so that the smoke billows into the makeshift smokehouse. It should take you about a day to get a week or so worth of meat preserved this way, though if you are able to smoke for 2 straight days, you should have enough for a month. The meat is done when it is completely dried all the way through from the smoke.

Storing Your Preserved Meat

Anytime you preserve meat, you need to store it properly and safely. Preserved meat should be stored 100 yards away from your cook site, and your campsite. You can easily form a triangle shape with 100 yards between each corner of the triangle. This will keep animals away from your cook site and ensure that your cookware is unlikely to become bothered.

Store your meat in a double or even triple wrapped bag with fabric and tarp, and if you can, layer charcoal from the campfire between two of the layers to attempt to mask some of the scents of your meat. Then, tie it all up in a big sack and hang that sack out on the end of a large branch. You want the sack to be high enough off the ground that animals cannot reach up to it, and low enough off the branch that animals cannot reach down to it. You also want the area to be clear enough that you can easily keep an eye on everything around you when you are accessing your meat, so you are unlikely to be interrupted and harmed.

Use a large rope to store your meat by tying it to the sack, throwing it over a large branch, and tugging on the rope to pull the sack up toward the branch. Then, secure the end of the rope around the trunk of the tree itself with a knot or a toggle to keep it safely in place until you release it and drop the bag down again for you to access your food with.

CHAPTER 8

Hygiene And Medicine

Hygiene is always important, but it becomes even more important when you are living in the bush. Without proper hygiene, you run the risk of catching an illness and finding yourself in a dangerous or even fatal situation, rapidly. Knowing how to practice proper bush medicine is important, as it ensures that should anything go wrong, you will be able to treat it the best you possibly can. Fortunately, although you may not have access to immediate medical services, there are many things you can do in the bush to help take care of yourself and keep yourself as healthy as possible. In this chapter, we will cover basic bush hygiene and medicine, as well as what to do in the event of common minor injuries.

Personal Hygiene In the Bush

Having a proper hygiene kit for the bush is important. Your hygiene kit should include a toothbrush and toothpaste, a hairbrush, nail clippers, a file, small scissors, a bar of unscented soap, and a razor if you are a male as it will allow you to shave your face if needed. Small cloths that can be used for wiping yourself down and a hand towel are great to have, too.

Every day you should focus on brushing your teeth, brushing your hair, and keeping up with your usual washing routine. However, you should refrain from using soap to wash on a regular basis as doing so can change your scent and make you easier for animals to track. This can make predators curious, and prey fearful, putting you in a bad position in the bush.

Feet are the most important part of hygiene, especially in the bush. When you are bushcrafting, they are put through a lot, from sitting in boots all the time to being rubbed around and exposed to rough terrain as you engage in all the tasks you need to in order to stay healthy and safe. Feet can get small abrasions, bruises, cuts, and blisters. Any of these can quickly fester into serious injuries if you are not careful, so you must always keep your feet as clean as you possibly can. You must also keep your feet dry as wet feet can rapidly develop fungi, which can turn into sores and, as you can probably guess, serious injuries.

If you find yourself unable to access any hygienic products before you leave for the bush, or if you run out, there are a few things you can use in the bush to help you. The smoke from campfires is actually incredibly useful and can be used to wash. Standing in the smoke and letting it get exposed to all parts of you helps neutralize any bacteria that may be lingering anywhere on you and sanitizes your skin and any clothes you may expose to the smoke, too.

You can also use the charcoal from the fire pit to wash your hands and brush your teeth. Or, you can find the bark of a dogwood or a sassafras tree, both of which are quite fibrous and are high in tannic acid. The heightened tannins mean that these two trees are great for cleaning your teeth as they will eliminate any bacteria. Plus, the fibrous nature of them means they can actually scrub your teeth and eliminate any build-up from your mouth.

If using charcoal to wash your hands is not an option or not ideal for you in this moment, you can also use a plant that is high in saponins, which are anti-bacterial and commonly found in everyday soap products. Saponins are readily found in plants like yucca, which are fibrous and excellent for scrubbing hands with.

Which Trees and Plants Are Useful

In the bush, there are many plants you will come across that can help you in different ways. Pines, willow and poplars, black walnut, sassafras, and oaks are all the most likely to give you the best results and are found abundantly nearly everywhere you go. You should also look up a local herbalism guide which will indicate which local flora is useful in medical situations, or in different situations you may encounter in the book. This way, you are educated on plant life in your area, and you can use it as needed.

In the bush, pine trees are great for firewood and building. However, they are also great for medical situations. The sap from pine trees is astringent, antiseptic, anti-inflammatory, and antibacterial. Applying it to wounds helps clean them out and behaves like super glue to hold your wound together. It can also be used to stop bleeding, treat rashes, and to treat sore throats.

The bark of willow trees contains salicin, which turns into salicylic acid in the body. Salicylic acid is great for treating minor aches and pains, arthritis, headaches, and muscle soreness because it acts as an anti-inflammatory. It is especially helpful if you are not particularly used to the demands of bushcraft and find yourself aching at the end of the day, or the next morning.

Poplars are available year-round, making them an excellent tree to rely on. They are easy to spot and can help with an array of things. A poultice made from the leaves of poplar can be used for inflammation and sores; the inner bark can be made into a tea for fevers or upset stomachs; the inner bark can also be chewed if you have a toothache, and it can be used to treat coughs and worms. The easiest way to use poplar is as a tea or a tonic.

Black walnut is great for its ability to kill germs, making it excellent for astringent and antiseptic purposes. Turn it into a poultice to treat a poison ivy rash, or steep it in water to turn it into a wash that will kill bacteria.

Sassafras expels digestive gas, making it an excellent tree to turn into a tea if you are dealing with digestive disorders. The bark itself is also loaded with vitamin C, making it excellent for a natural immune boost in the bush. It can also be turned into a poultice for wounds or rashes. Be careful not to ingest too much sassafras, however, as it can be poisonous in high quantities.

Oaks are the best for building, but they are also great for medicinal situations. White oak in particular, has been used for thousands of years as a medicine. The inner bark is taken from the tree, ground, and decocted to treat any ailment above the neck, ranging from a stuffed nose to a sore throat or a headache. It can also help you prevent excess fluid leakage from the body, meaning it is excellent for runny noses, or if you are dealing with diarrhea. As well, the inner bark of an oak tree can be boiled into a tea and used to clean off wounds before treating them.

Always use the healthiest looking trees available, as they will have the best to offer when it comes to medicinal value. Turn any medicine into a decoction or infusion and consume 8 ounces 3 to 4 times per day, as needed.

Treating Wounds In the Bush

In the bush, treating a wound is vital. Shallow wounds should be first cleaned with an astringent like black walnut or oak; then it should be coated with either honey if you were able to bring any, or fresh pine resin. Get the resin out of the center of the tree, rather than the sap that has been expelled from the tree, as this will be the cleanest kind. Slightly heat it over a fire to make it gooey enough to cover a wound with.

If you have a deep wound, you may need to sew it shut. In this case, you will first clean it, then sew it with a needle that has been sterilized in the fire, and then dress it with pine resin. You will want to cover it with a clean cloth and change the dressing every four to six hours to prevent an infection from developing in the wound.

Dealing With Broken Digits or Limbs

Broken digits or limbs in the bush can be terribly painful and challenging to deal with. Digits are much less of a hassle to deal with as they are not quite as large, and, generally, there is not much you can do for them. If your digit is bent in the wrong direction, you will first need to set it, which means you will need to bend it back in the right direction. As soon as you have, it should find its way back into place. After you have done this, you will want to take a straight, sturdy little branch that is the length of your finger if one of the last two joints was broken, or the length of your hand from your wrist to the tip of your finger if the base joint was broken. Then, you will use a strip of fabric to bind your broken finger to the branch, keeping the branch *over* your hand, not under the palm, to avoid cutting yourself with the end of it whenever you bend your wrist. Keep it this way until the finger is healed.

With arms or legs, you are going to want to evacuate from the bush and seek medical treatment as quickly as possible as these larger bones can rapidly pose a serious threat to anyone who has them. The best way to deal with the broken bone in the field is to cover it with a folded blanket or other soft padded item and carefully tie that item around the broken limb. Then, you will carefully make your way back to civilization, where you can seek support in dealing with that broken limb. Never try to heal a broken limb on your own as they can easily become infected, and if they are set wrong, they can remain damaged for life with no chance of properly healing. In some cases, the limb may no longer be useful or may have to be amputated if it is not set and healed properly.

Healing Gastrointestinal Illness In the Bush

Gastrointestinal illness may mean a day in bed when you are at home, but in the bush, it can rapidly become dangerous. Vomiting and diarrhea can expel much-needed hydration from your body, causing you to rapidly become dehydrated and at risk of fatal illness. This is why people died of grippe before standard medicine protocol was invented. Sassafras infusions should be drank 3-4 times a day in 8-ounce increments, and the ill individual should do their best to continue sipping water throughout the entire day. White oak infusions can also be drunk for diarrhea to hopefully help calm things down and prevent further illness. They should also try to get bites of dried protein whenever possible, as this will ensure that they are able to keep themselves hydrated and nourished. Always thoroughly clean the camp after anyone has been ill to avoid having illness lingering. As well, you will want to be particularly cautious as animals tend to be more aware of other ill mammals based on scent and can become more of a danger when someone is ill.

CHAPTER 9

Leveraging The Environment

Knowing how to use the environment to your benefit is one of the best ways to secure your survival in the bush. The environment can be used in a myriad of ways to support you with survival, whether it be offering food for you to consume or a safe place for you to find shelter. The best way to learn how to leverage the environment is to educate yourself on your local environment and get to know what it is like around you. Pay close attention to what the geography and landscaping are usually like, to what types of plants and animals exist in the area, and to what type of phenomena happen in your area. Knowing how to leverage the environment will go a long way in helping you survive because it ultimately makes survival easier. When you know what to look for, you are able to let the land do much of the work for your survival while you simply have to fill in the gaps.

Educating Yourself On Local Plant Life

The first and biggest thing you can do for yourself is to educate yourself on local plant life. Every area has its own form of vegetation that contributes to the ecosystem, and that can be used in different ways. Educating yourself on the flora local to your environment ensures that you are able to get accurate information on plants that will be relevant for you.

The best way to start educating yourself on local plant life is to invest in a plant guide that is relevant to your local area. Begin reading through it and recognizing which plants are most popular in your area, then highlight them. You do not need to know every single flora in your area, nor do you need to know how all of it works. However, you do need to know the ones that are going to be most likely to help you. Look for flora that can be safely consumed, as well as flora that can be used for medical purposes for treating injuries and for treating illnesses. You should have a few different plants identified for each circumstance. Next, get out in the field and practice identifying those plants so that you can see them for yourself and get comfortable with identifying them and locating them in the wild. This way, if you are ever caught in a survival situation, it is easy for you to locate what you need.

If you want to feel even more confident in your local flora, you can always work with a herbalist. Local herbalists are educated in local flora and vegetation, and therefore they have an abundance of information and answers on local plant life. Many will offer plant walks in nearby forests and parks and, on those walks, will help you confidently identify important plants. They can also educate you on how to safely and sustainably harvest those plants and use them if need be, and you can ask as many questions as you need or want.

Properly and Safely Identifying Plants

It is important that you learn to properly and safely identify any plants you are considering using, as many plants are known for having plants that look similar but are highly poisonous. For example, grapes are safe to consume, but pokeweed berries that look like greats are toxic and become even more toxic as they mature, to the point where consumption can be fatal. Never eat just anything you see, and always be absolutely confident that what you are eating is safe to eat.

The best way to properly and safely identify plants is to practice doing so, especially with the guide of someone with greater skill who can confirm one way or another if you have properly identified said plant. Going out in the field with someone who knows what they are talking about means that they can help you recognize certain signs or indications that allow you to tell a safe plant apart from a dangerous one. You should do this several times over and keep notes in your local plant life book if need be to ensure that you are prepared to safely and confidently identify the local flora in a survivalist situation if need be.

Another way to protect yourself is to educate yourself on the poisonous plants in your area, and any poisonous plants that tend to look like the ones you intend to rely on if you find yourself in a survivalist situation. As they say, "keep your friends close, but your enemies closer." The better you are at identifying dangerous plants, the less likely you will be to accidentally engage with them and find yourself ill or even dead as a result.

Consuming and Storing Edible Plants

Most plants that are edible can be consumed as is, though some may taste better when cooked. In a survivalist setting, you can harvest plant matter directly from a plant itself, though it is important to do so in a sustainable way. Harvesting plant matter in a sustainable way ensures that you are able to continue harvesting from the same plant over and over and that you do not slowly deplete any given area of a certain type of plant. Typically, plants should be harvested above the root and near any "joints" that you may see in the leaves or stems.

All harvested plants should be washed in fresh, filtered water, as you never know what has been on or around that plant. Animal urine can contaminate plants and transfer bacteria and parasites onto them, rendering them dangerous for you to eat. If you are picking from a bush, always pick high up where the plant is likely to remain less bothered by animals. Practice care when harvesting to avoid being bitten or stung by an insect that could be harmful in and of itself.

If you are not going to consume something right away, store it in a clean, dry, cool space for up to a couple of days. Berries, for example, could be stored inside of a loosely sealed container in the shade or in a shallow, cool stream. Green plant matter can either be dried and used to season meats or other foods with or can be stored in the same manner as berries would be until you are ready to consume them.

Using the Landscape to Build a Camp

Aside from using local vegetation for medicine and food, there are other ways to use the landscape to your advantage. One great way is to use the landscape itself to help you build a camp. While you do need to watch for the 5 W's, it is helpful to use the landscape to help you in as many ways as possible. Avoid setting up camp "just anywhere" and set camp up somewhere that is already relatively cleared out, or that has something you can use for setting up camp. Look for trees that are the right height, branches that are going to allow you to easily hang things, and water that is easy to access and clean.

When it comes to your survival, the last thing you want to have to worry about is trying to clear out a proper campsite so that you can access everything you need. Having to cut away trees, clear out brush, or clean off the dirt itself so that you can use the landscape properly requires work, and work uses up calories, and calories are harder to come by in the bush. You need to preserve as much of your energy and time as you possibly can so that you are able to use it on other, more important things such as finding water and food and keeping yourself warm, hydrated, and fed.

Another thing you should consider when you are getting ready to set up camp is how easy it will be to set your food preservation site and cook site up. A well-placed camp should be able to be a part of a triangle, with your cook site and your food preservation site all kept 100 yards apart. If you are going to have to climb any nasty hills or do any excessive or treacherous walking to get to these areas, you are going to find yourself at greater risk. You want to try to find an area that is going to be easy to live in and navigate so that you can make it as effortless as possible for you to survive. As it is, survival is going to take more energy and effort than you can possibly imagine. The easier you can make it for yourself, the better.

Getting Creative With the Landscape

Speaking of making things easier through the landscape, it can be helpful to look for other ways to make use of the landscape, too. More often than not, the earth is formed in such a way that it can effortlessly help us achieve anything we desire, whether that be to create shelter, hunt or prepare food, or gather water for drinking, cleaning, and cooking.

Before you embark on any survival venture, stop and survey the landscape. What do you see? What might be able to help you make your job easier? How might you be able to achieve more with less? Consider looking for trees that are already perfectly shaped to help you set up your tarp or tent, or for branches that are already the perfect height for you to prepare your game. Look for parts of the water that are easy to access or runways that are already made so that you can easily move around the forest you are currently residing in.

When we spend our entire lives in urban environments, it can be easy to forget that nature itself has its own system going on inside of it. When you step into that system, there is no need to reinvent it or try to manipulate it to be your way. Doing so will only use up your energy and make it more challenging for you to survive. Focus instead on meshing into the system that already exists and using it to your advantage. Get creative. Look for ways to make things work, and don't be afraid to make adaptations as needed. One of the greatest survival skills anyone can have is the ability to adapt their plans as needed and shift into a system that works for their present situation. When you know how to get creative and make things work for what you need, you increase your chances of survival tenfold.

CONCLUSION

Surviving in the bush will not be the easiest task you will ever come up against, should you find yourself in this situation. There are many challenges you will face, many hardships you will have to overcome, and many adaptations you will need to make. If you do find yourself in a survival situation, one thing I want to warn you against is what will likely be the greatest challenge you will face. That is, your mind.

Your mind is a wildly powerful tool, and when it is fixed to help you survive, it will do wonders. However, your mind can and will go through phases where it seems virtually impossible for you to survive at all. You are going to wonder if it is worth it, what you are doing this for, and if it is even possible for you to survive in the long run. You may become anxious from all of the changes and stress, depressed from all of the loss, or angry from everything you are being faced with. This is all normal and natural. You must learn to ride the natural waves of your emotions while still charging forward if you are going to survive, and you must learn how to always put your survival above anything else.

This book is an excellent resource to help you learn how to survive in the bush, but the truth of the matter is that your memory is not going to function the same under the stress of a survivalist situation. You would be best to keep a printed copy of this safely tucked into your grab and go bag so that if you do find yourself in the bush, you also have access to all of the information right here in these pages. One small mistake in the bush can be dangerous and even fatal, so having this available to keep you on top of things is important.

I also encourage you to keep going from here. Do not make this the only way you educate yourself for survival. Keep researching, reading, and looking to understand everything you can. You can start by checking out my other titles, *Survival 101: Beginner's Guide 2020, Survival 101: Food Storage,* and *Survival 101: Raised Bed Gardening.* There are many guides out there, all of which will give you valuable information to help you discover exactly what you need to know in order to survive. Be sure to research your locale, as well, to discover what your terrain is like, where the best areas for setting up camp are, and how to survive once you get there. The more you can educate yourself on local threats and risks, the easier it will be for you to prepare yourself and protect yourself if you ever find yourself in a situation where you need to.

Before you go, I ask that you please take a moment to review *Survival 101: Bushcraft* on Amazon Kindle. Your honest feedback would be greatly appreciated, as it will help others like you discover how they, too, can survive in the bush. It will also help me write more great titles for you.

Thank you, and good luck! Stay safe out there.

DESCRIPTION

Surviving a wild situation seems like a hefty task, but what if it is inevitable?

Have you ever found yourself wondering how you would fare in the bush?

Do you worry about what might happen if you find yourself having to evacuate the safety of your home due to an emergency? Could you survive it? Wonder no more.

The reality is, survival is a task we are all faced with in life. At times, however, we may be faced with surviving under less than stellar conditions. In our modern society, we have become so accustomed to having all of our survival needs met that the idea of having to meet them ourselves seems... *impossible*. It doesn't have to be.

The truth is, you are wired to survive. But that doesn't mean it would be easy to survive in the wilderness. Not growing up in the face of exposure means that you may be entirely unaware of what to look for, what to avoid, where to find food and water, what methods to use to sterilize that food and water, or how to navigate surviving the wilderness. It's time you change that.

Survival 101: Bushcraft, The Essential Guide for Wilderness Survival 2020, was written to help you discover how you should navigate the wilderness to help you survive any situation you come across. While this book may be enjoyable for hobbyists, its geared toward those of you who are ready to discover what it takes to actually *survive*. The contents of this book will walk you through the step by step process of discovering how to survive any situation you are faced with, with ease.

The contents of this book are written in order based on everything you need to know to survive. From procuring shelter to securing food and water and protecting yourself from predators, illness, or injury, everything you need to know is carefully stored inside these pages.

Some of what you will discover in *Survival 101: Bushcraft* include:

- What skills and tools are essential to your survival
- How to set up a secure campground, including where to place your cooking and food facilities for safety
- How to build and manage a fire
- Essential navigation and tracking skills, including how to find yourself if you are lost
- Methods for securing food and water, including how to butcher game meat
- How to cook, preserve, and store any game you trap
- Necessary hygiene and medicine practices to know in the bush, including which plants you can rely on for medicinal purposes, and how
- How to leverage the environment around you for easier survival
- And more!

This book is an excellent guide for anyone, anywhere; however, it will show you how to specifically tailor your survival to your environment. Buy your copy of *Survival 101: Bushcraft, The Essential Guide for Wilderness Survival 2020* today to discover how you can prepare yourself to survive in the wilderness. With the way things are going these days, you will be glad you did!

CPSIA information can be obtained
at www.ICGtesting.com
Printed in the USA
LVHW011642201021
700968LV00003B/275